ONLINE LEARNING MADE EASY AND EFFECTIVE

Terris R. Moss, PhD

Copyright © 2020 Terris R. Moss

All rights reserved. No part of this book may be reproduced or used in any manner without the prior written permission of the copyright owner, except for the use of brief quotations in a book review.

To request permission, contact the publisher at info@mossconsultingllc.com

ISBN: 978-1-7350011-0-4

Printed by Infinity Publishing in the USA
Legacy Publishing
Ewing, NJ 08618

Dedication

This book is dedicated to my departed mother, Christine Virginia Cozart. Thank you for everlasting love and belief in my greatness even when I did not believe in myself

Acknowledgement

To my husband, Leon and my son, Terrel, thank you for being such a big part of my personal growth. My sister thank you for helping me with making sure everything was printed professionally. Without all of you, I would not be the person I am today. And to the rest of my family, extended family and friends, and those who have supported all of my endeavors, I sincerely thank you for all your support and encouragement.

About the Author

Terris Rene Moss, PhD, President of Moss Consulting, LLC, is one of the nation's top online learning strategists. Dr. Moss provides speaking and coaching services to online degree program students and educators. Her academic history includes teaching online graduate courses in Clinical Research Science, Project Management, Regulatory and Ethics courses as Faculty Instructor at Rutgers University, School of Health Professions and as an Adjunct Assistant Professor at George Washington University Clinical Research Leadership program. During Dr. Moss' academic career, her accomplishments have included using innovative methods to produce effective learning experiences including cooperative learning. In addition to academia, Dr. Moss' training expertise in corporate training includes developing educational-based training programs in good clinical practices, medical writing, and project management which enhance the learning experiences of multiple types of learners including visual, auditory, reading/writing, and kinesthetic.

Table of Contents

Dedication	iii
Acknowledgement	iv
About the Author	v
Introduction	2
Chapter 1: What Is Online Learning? Myths Debunked, Pros and Cons	**5**
Three Myths Debunked	7
Truths about Online Learning	11
Synchronous and Asynchronous Learning	14
Accreditation	16
Blended Learning	17
How Do Online College Classes Work?	17
Chapter 2: Benefit of Online Learning	**20**
Flexibility	21
Reduced Costs	22

More Choices of Courses and Programs	23
Networking, Diversity and Professional Growth Opportunities	24
Increased Time with the Instructor	25
Access to Expertise	26
Easier to Focus	27
You Can Keep Your Job	28
Learning New Tech Skills	28
Chapter 3: Challenges Students May Face with Online Learning	**30**
Self-Discipline and Responsibility	30
Refined Critical-Thinking Skills	31
Technical Skills	31
Lack of Social Interaction	32
Some Online Courses Can Be Boring	33
Chapter 4: Determining If Online Learning Is for You	**35**
Characteristics of an Effective Online Learner	35
Strategies for Staying Motivated to Complete the Online Learning Program	38
Student Online Assessment of Readiness	40
Online Program Readiness Assessment Quiz 1	42
Online Program Readiness Assessment Quiz 2	46
Interpreting the Results	51

Chapter 5: Choosing an
Online Learning Program — 53

Managing Online Education Expectations — 54

Ensuring a Quality Education — 56

How long has the online college been around? — 57

Is the college or university accredited? — 57

Does the online degree
program accept transfer credits? — 61

Is the school in a good financial position? — 62

Are there any hidden costs? — 67

What is the cost and average student debt? — 68

Can the degree program
help you reach your career goals? — 69

Are the online courses best in class? — 70

What type of academic, career, and
technical support is available to online students? — 71

Chapter 6: Discussion Boards — 74

What Is a Discussion Board Post? — 75

Strategies and Tips for Discussion Board Postings — 78

Common Online Discussion Board
Pitfalls and How to Avoid Them — 86

Discussion Board Student Checklist. — 88

Chapter 7: Learning Management Systems — 91

What Are Learning Management Systems? — 91

What Is the Primary Function of the LMS? — 93

Features of Learning Managements Systems	95
Types of Learning Management Systems	97

Chapter 8: Determine Your Learning Style — 101

What Is a Learning Style?	101
Benefits of Identifying Your Predominant Learning Style	103
VARK Theory	105
Other Indexes for Determining Learning Style	106
The Index of Learning Styles	108
Learning Styles Self-Assessment	110

Chapter 9: Learning Styles and Study Strategies — 115

Visual Learning Style	115
Strategies for the Visual Learning Student (learns best by seeing)	118
Specific Strategies of Visual Learners for Studying	119
How Best to Work with Teachers	121
Auditory Learning Style	124
Strategies for the Auditory Learner (learns best by hearing)	127
Tactile Learner or Kinesthetic Learner	127
Strategies for the Kinesthetic Learner (learns best by doing "hands on")	129

Chapter 10: Time Management Tips for the Online Student — 133

Why Do Online Students Need Time Management? — 134

Can Anyone Learn to Manage Their Time Better? — 135

Learning Simple Time Management — 136

How to Manage Your Commuting Time to Improve Your eLearning — 137

Time Management - Final Thoughts — 139

Discussion Board Posting Time Management - Sample of Typical Week — 141

Chapter 11: Strategies for the Online Learner — 143

Front-Load Your Work — 143

Ask Lots of Questions — 144

Release Your Extrovert — 144

Perception Can Be Your (Virtual) Reality — 145

Get a Support System of Family and Friends — 145

Stay Connected — 146

Have an Open Mind — 147

Hold Yourself Accountable — 147

Chapter 12: Strategies, Hacks and Resources for Online Learning Success — 150

Tip 1 – Treat Studying Like a Job — 150

Tip 2 – Make Use of Online Resources — 151

Tip 3 – Check in Daily — 152

Tip 4 – Don't Multitask	152
Tip 5 – Speak Up and Ask Questions	153
Tip 6 – Connect with Others	154
Tip 7 – Join a Study Team	155
Tip 8 – Set Up Your Virtual Office	156
Tip 9 – Embrace Project Management Tools	157
Conclusion	**159**
Resources for Online Education Students	**162**

This book is for . . .

- Students who are enrolled or considering enrolling in an online program at an educational institution

- Academic program directors, chairs, administrators and faculty who lead online degree programs, as this book can serve as an orientation to online learning

- Teachers and instructors of online degree programs

- Students who wish to learn the nuances of learning management systems

- Students who want to identify their individual learning style and study strategies based on their style of learning

- Potential students and teachers who want to improve engagement with peers and faculty of online programs

"Online learning is rapidly becoming one of the most cost-effective ways to education the world's rapidly expanding workforce"

Jack Messman, Former CEO at Novell, Cambridge Technology Partners, Union Pacific Resources, Somerset House Corp.

Introduction

Terris R. Moss, one of the nation's top online learning strategists, is passionate about expanding enriching education opportunities to multiple types of learners and at-risk populations. Dr. Moss developed this resource for college students or parents of college students who are undertaking online courses to provide a foundation for appropriately navigating online programs and distilling any myths or beliefs. One common misconception is that online courses are easier; however, as online students are often working full or part time, sometimes while raising a family, completing an online course while managing personal obligations requires thoughtful time management and discipline.

The purpose of this resource is to give students an overview of the types of online learning, suggest basic

Introduction

strategies (tips) to complete an online program successfully and provide a list of resources available to help navigate through managing the nuances and differences in studying and completing an online course. Learning style concept is introduced as a way for the reader to gain insight in their own learning style and accompanying study strategies. It is Dr. Moss' hope that the reader will find these strategies helpful in completing their online course as well as open the door to online learning as an option for your future educational goals. Dr. Moss and her team welcome the opportunity to be a future resource for the reader should you decide online learning is right for you.

"Online learning helps eliminate physical and social barriers for obtaining a high quality education"

Terris R. Moss, PhD, Educator, Author, Speaker

1

What Is Online Learning? Myths Debunked, Pros and Cons

Thanks to the rapid advancement of technology, online learning is a part of many institutions' course offerings around the world. From certificates to PhDs, impactful online language learning and everything in between, learning online has never been so accessible. Offered by some of the world's top-ranked institutions, online learning offers students all the perks of attending their dream university with the added convenience of a learning experience tailored to their schedule. With courses available in almost every subject and flexible timetables to suit almost every lifestyle, students are increasingly turning to online learning as a viable alternative to on-campus study. It can allow you to study abroad remotely, at a university not in your home country. Advances in technology now allow students to study entirely online while still socializing with classmates, watching lectures and participating in subject-specific discussions.

While some consider online learning to require a greater degree of self-motivation, institutions recognize that educational support is just as important as tutor feedback and take great care to ensure that their students receive the same levels of support that they would receive on campus.

Online learning is the future of education as it offers flexibility to the teacher and the student to set their own learning pace and a schedule that fits everyone's agenda. As a result, using an online educational platform allows for a better balance of work and studies, so there's no need to give anything up. Having a common agenda between the student and teacher can also prompt both parties to accept new responsibilities and have more autonomy.

Today's online courses offer a variety of skills and subjects to learn. Online platforms called Learning Management Systems, or LMS, offer courses for various levels and disciplines, and the growing popularity of online education has led to more and more courses bursting onto the scene. From guitar lessons to quantum physics, there are options for every type of student so there's no reason to give up working or studying while exploring new and exotic places as students' online content is available at any moment from anywhere.

THREE MYTHS DEBUNKED

There are many misconceptions of exactly what online learning is and what it is not. Three common misconceptions are that online courses are easier, the quality is lower, and instructors are not available.

MYTH 1: ONLINE EDUCATION IS EASY.

Unfortunately some students sign up for online courses in the belief that they will be able to sail through coursework. But, as anyone who has ever received a take-home test knows, instructors often compensate for the availability of resources by increasing expectations.

Online classes demand every bit as much time and attention as in-class lessons. They often include more written correspondence with teachers and classmates as well as extra quizzes or written coursework to measure progress. Students who underestimate the workload risk falling behind.

Students must realize that it is not easier to earn a degree online than in a traditional brick-and-mortar setting. It is just a different way of learning. Students may have more flexibility as to when they study, but the flexibility comes with challenges. Students will have to complete the same material as in-person, except they also must manage their time because no one is reminding them when their work is due. Online courses require more self-direction than traditional courses where face-to-face instructors are available. Online students who are working full or part time, while often raising a family, and completing an online course while managing personal obligations will need to develop thoughtful time management and discipline.

MYTH 2: THE QUALITY IS LOWER.

While academic standards for online courses may vary from school to school, online schools and faculties go through the same accreditation and rigorous certification processes as brick-and-mortar schools. Since online education has become more widely accepted, many accredited institutions have included online courses as part of their curriculum. In fact, it is increasingly unusual for today's college students to graduate without ever having taken an online course.

But it's not just higher education that offers accredited courses. More private educators have taken steps to gain accreditation for their courses, thereby increasing their value. Furthermore, the routes these educators need to take to gain accreditation are rigorous, which is a reminder that just because the program is online does not mean it's easy to obtain.

In fact, it has been Dr. Moss' experience as a former assistant professor that online schools required her to communicate differently to teach scientific concepts my online students. Dr. Moss had to think about effectiveness and engagement far more actively and doing so made her a better instructor.

Myth 3: Online students
cannot meet with the instructor.

While it is true that many students have found online courses to be more isolating than classrooms, the isolation can be partly attributed to poor course design rather than an inherent flaw in online education. Although it might be impossible for students to physically be in the same place as their instructors, there are opportunities for meaningful interactions. How much interaction is up to the instructor as certainly there are courses where the teacher operates in the background and students essentially follow the formula and learn on their own. However, most online classrooms also provide the opportunity for instructors to join in on discussion room chats, offer webinars, or even conduct video chats with students who need more personal guidance. For private instructors, these are also unique selling points that can be used to boost the value of the course. Students will have opportunities to interact with their professors by various means including phone, email or Skype, video conferences, and online chat sessions. Online faculty usually has online office hours each week where students can make appointments. Discussion forums, online collaborative projects, and group webinars are all positive ways fellow students can interact with each other during an online course. While it can be awkward for students to break the ice, with the right incentives many students find they're more confident when expressing themselves in writing rather than in person. This may make online education a more comfortable way for introverts to bond with their classmates than traditional classrooms.

So now that the myths are debunked, we should discuss what online learning is.

TRUTHS ABOUT ONLINE LEARNING

In a traditional classroom, you often learn by listening, reading, writing, and doing other activities designed by your instructor. Online courses are different because you are not in the same location as your instructor or the other students. In fact, you probably will never meet your instructor or fellow students in person. In online courses, students "attend" class by visiting the class web pages. They complete assignments according to the class schedule. Students communicate with the instructor and classmates using email and online discussion forums.

This class format is very flexible for busy schedules. Students can often log on to the course at any time of the day (or night). Computer skills and determination are necessary to be successful. Students need keyboarding skills and must be able to write so that others can understand.

There are many misconceptions of what exactly online learning is and what it is not. Online learning is education that takes place over the internet. It is often referred to as "e-learning", or "distance learning" among other terms. Quite simply, online learning is the umbrella term for any learning that takes place across distance and not in a traditional classroom.

Online learning programs are conducted in various formats including:

- Self-study – The reader is often provided textbooks or other study materials to learn on their own or with some remote guidance. In self-study, competency and comprehension of knowledge is tested through manual or electronic means.

- Video/audio tape – Creation of training videos and/or audio recordings to train the student.

- Web-based trainings – The student typically logs into a website to access training course content.

- Blended eLearning /Instructor-led – Colleges sometimes offer a blended format where there is an instructor who leads and directs students through the online learning course content. Students are typically accountable to complete and demonstrate competency in learning during a set time frame. This online learning format is most popular with online degree programs.

- Mobile learning – A newer form of e-learning in which education or training is conducted by means of portable computing devices such as smartphones or tablets.

Online education and degree programs have grown over the last few years and have experienced mainstream acceptance. An Online Education Trend Report published in the *Journal on E-Learning* included questions about perceptions of online education in a student survey. Basically, learners were asked if they think online education is better than, equal to, or inferior to on-campus education. Responses to the survey indicated that a majority of students feel that online learning is "better than" or "equal to" on-campus learning. When the students were asked about their employers' perceptions, the results were similar. The Online Educational Trend Report suggested a new trend for online learning student demographics as the majority of students seeking online education were doing so as a means for career acceleration and earning an academic credential in a field where they already work or have practical experience. There is a pronounced demand for online education, especially among adult learners, and now the norm is about 33 percent of college students are taking at least one course online. Top areas for academic growth in online programs are healthcare, business, computer science, education, faith-based programs and lastly general studies. Survey responders agreed with an online class, the learner has more control over their learning environment and increased opportunities to tailor the learner's education into something that fits them, not the other way around.

Synchronous and Asynchronous Learning

There are fundamentally two types of e-learning that need to be discussed; they are Synchronous training and Asynchronous training. Synchronous means "at the same time"; therefore this training includes interaction of participants with an instructor via the web in real time. The instructor has a virtual classroom online where other students and learners interact with each other and instructors through instant messaging chat, audio and video conferencing, etc. Sessions are recorded and can be accessed during the course. The benefits of synchronous learning are:

- Having the ability to log or track learning activities through recorded sessions.

- Instructors provide continuous monitoring and provide immediate correction if needed.

- Opens the possibilities of global connectivity and collaboration opportunities among learners.

- Assists the instructor with personalizing the training for each learner.

Synchronous e-learning is used when instructor-based online mentoring is best suited for students who may need concept-based training and help with their regular studies. With this type of learning, there is a constant interaction between instructor and student in which the instructor can explain complex concepts through examples and clarification of doubts.

Asynchronous, which means "not at the same time," allows the participants to complete web-based training at their own pace, without live interaction with the instructor. The course materials are available on a self-access basis 24/7. The advantage of asynchronous learning is that the student has access to the information they need whenever they need it. Asynchronous learning includes interaction amongst participants through message boards, bulletin boards and discussion forums. Additional advantages of asynchronous learning include:

- Course material is available "just in time" for instant learning and reference.

- The student has flexibility of access from anywhere at any time.

- The instructor can simultaneously reach an unlimited number of students.

- The course material is uniformly delivered to the users.

Asynchronous e-learning methods are used in different situations, usually when the topics are generic and business-related such as management training, financial training, time management, etc. Courses that need extensive simulations are also good candidates for asynchronous techniques where virtual classroom teaching is not required and training material does not change often. Process-based training is best handled through the asynchronous method where the student gets prerecorded study material that he studies in his own time and can post his queries to message boards, bulletin boards, discussion sites, seminars, etc. The clear advantage of a self-paced course is convenience. Students can get the training they need at any time allowing for a greater degree of flexibility.

ACCREDITATION

Accreditation standards are the same for online learning. Accredited programs, whether on-campus or online, must have the approval of an accrediting agency, which means any accredited online program meets the same standards as accredited on-campus options. Students can search for schools through the U.S. Department of Education's website to determine accreditation status. More information on Accreditation is available in Chapter 5 – Choosing an Online Learning Program.

BLENDED LEARNING

Most university online programs will have blended learning, which is a combination of synchronous and asynchronous learning methods. Using both online training through virtual classrooms and giving CDs and study material for self-study is now being increasingly preferred over any single type of training.

HOW DO ONLINE COLLEGE CLASSES WORK?

Learning Management Systems, or LMS, allow instructors to upload course information for easy student access. Common learning management systems include Blackboard, Canvas, and Moodle, which provide accessible exchange of information between professors and students. If the department delivers a course asynchronously, degree candidates may view lectures and course materials, such as PowerPoint presentations and syllabi, at a time convenient for them. Synchronous courses, however, require scheduled attendance through online chats or video conferencing tools such as Zoom.

Students submit course assignments through a learning management system by posting on discussion forums and submitting tasks through applicable links. To submit a research paper, for example, a student using Blackboard could click on the assignment link to upload the finished product. Instructors may provide feedback to the student through comments or email.

Student coursework will be similar between traditional and online courses, with students having to complete exams, papers, presentations, quizzes and projects on a syllabus. Online students typically submit forum posts to engage in peer discussion, which acts as a substitute for in-person class attendance. Weekly readings and course lectures surface in both delivery methods, supplying on-campus and distance students with solid course information. This combination makes online learning both effective and engaging.

Online courses require just as much work and time requirements as traditional in-house courses. Each week, your instructor typically expects you to take the following actions yourself:

1. Review the learning objectives

2. Complete the assigned readings

3. Submit assignments

4. Go through the lecture materials

5. Participate in the discussion boards

"In times where small instructor-led classrooms tend to be the exception, electronic learning solutions can offer more collaboration and interaction with experts and peers as well as a higher success rate than the live alternative"

Keith Bachman, Corporate eLearning Executive, W.R. Hambrecht and Associates

2

Benefit of Online Learning

Current challenges facing traditional colleges and universities include higher tuition fees, budget cuts, and course shortages, which cause many students to search for alternatives. With nearly three million students currently enrolled in full time online programs and six million taking at least one online course as part of their degree, online education has clearly become one of the most popular higher education alternatives. The continually improving reputation of online learning has helped fuel its expansion, as initial skepticism faltered in the face of evidence showing that online learning can be just as effective as face-to-face education. Online education is preferred by individuals who may not be able to make it to classes in a traditional brick-and-mortar kind of college due to various reasons. Below we'll examine some of the benefits that online leaning education provides to its learners.

FLEXIBILITY

One of the most pronounced benefits of online learning is flexibility as students can choose the time and work environment that works best for them. With traditional classes, students have to work around the university schedule. If their class is at 4:00 p.m., they have to be in the classroom at that time and have to attend the entire lecture. Failing to do those things will result in missing valuable information. However, online classes make it so much easier for students to fit things into their schedule. Students can even watch part of a lecture, pause it, and then come back to it at a convenient time.

People who choose online learning tend to have other commitments and prefer this mode of learning as it gives them power over how they will delegate their time towards their different responsibilities. If the student is taking an asynchronous class or an online class, where they do not have to log in at a specific time for a live session, they have the flexibility to interact with their instructor and their fellow classmates at their own pace, usually through a discussion forum. Taking an online course also means that you do not have to commute to class and be subjected to weather conditions making it a challenge to attend class.

Additionally, online learning is beneficial for students who may not feel comfortable asking professors to repeat a point they made in their last lecture or dive into deeper detail on a specific topic; when learning online, students can revisit past material or stop the lecture to perform additional research or organize their notes. Students can work through the lesson plan at their own pace to ensure they are really mastering the material before moving on to the next section. This added flexibility allows online learners to move through the coursework at their own speed and get the most out of the degree program.

REDUCED COSTS

Online education often cost less than traditional schools due to a variety of reasons. As mentioned with the flexibility, there is no cost for commuting such as fuel, parking, car maintenance, and even public transportation costs will not affect the online student. Studying online means that students pay the tuition fee, book supplies, an online application fee, etc., but they do not incur the costs of housing, which could translate to lower debts and more savings.

More Choices of Courses and Programs

Studying online at the student's own convenience allows the student to no longer worry about class location when choosing what to learn next. By taking an online course, the student is able to focus on the subject they are interested in and choose from the options of many online courses and programs. An online college education may provide students access to specialized degree courses that may not be available in an easily accessible or local institution of learning. In addition, for students who want to attend summer classes but live too far from their colleges and/or work summer jobs, taking online classes from an accredited college and transferring the credits to their primary college can be beneficial. Students can earn college credit while still enjoying their summer vacation or fulfilling the responsibilities of their seasonal employment. Similarly, if a college or university does not offer enough open sections of a required course, students can take the course online at another college and transfer the credits.

Networking, Diversity and Professional Growth Opportunities

Students in online programs come from across the U.S. and all over the world. Because of the ability to log on from any location, class discussions feature a broader range of perspectives, helping you enhance your own cross-cultural understanding; online education provides students with the chance to network with other students across nations or even different continents. This often leads to other opportunities in terms of collaboration with other individuals in the implementation of a project. At the same time, students have an opportunity to learn culturally sensitivity, grow in their knowledge in working in a diverse culture, broaden their perspective, and become more culturally aware.

Learning to work with others in a virtual environment can make students more effective leaders. Students will develop critical leadership skills by utilizing specialized knowledge, creating efficient processes, and making decisions about best communication practices, such as what should be discussed in-person or electronically. Participating in discussion boards is a lot like participating in a virtual team. Communicating your ideas clearly, getting responses, and projecting a professional image are necessary skills in a virtual workplace.

Instructors, just like managers, expect you to write respectful, thoughtful, and polite communications, respond to different perspectives, and build a rapport with your peers. As students move through the program, they will get better at pitching their ideas and making strong, clear, professional arguments through text.

INCREASED TIME WITH THE INSTRUCTOR

Students in traditional classrooms may not get the personalized attention they need to have concepts clarified. In some ways, the distance is greater between you and your teacher because you're not sitting in class with them regularly. But in other ways, you have much easier access. When you ask a question in class, the professor has to consider other questions that need to be answered, the time it will take to answer the question and whether they even want to answer the question at all.

In an online class, you can email a teacher questions directly. When they answer, they can take as much time as they need to give you a thorough answer. They also don't have to worry about getting around to someone else's question before class ends. So in this way, you actually can have more of your professor's attention.

Most colleges have classes of students that number in the hundreds. This is not a problem for online education because online guided discussions and personal talk time with their professors and lecturers is a characteristic of online classes. This increases the chances of a student performing well due to the time their instructors give them. This also enhances their problem-solving and communication skills, as well as learning how to defend their arguments if needed.

ACCESS TO EXPERTISE

An online college education might give students access to specialized degree courses that may not be available in an easily accessible or local institution of learning. For example, at CCA you can pursue a degree in marketing or a certificate in C++ programming without having to live near the institution. Online classes allow for the sharing of expertise, which helps more people gain access to education that is not readily available in certain geographic locations.

This type of education has grown over the last few years and has experienced mainstream acceptance. With an online class, you get to control your learning environment, which ultimately helps you develop a deeper understanding of your degree course. New models of learning are always springing up in the market, providing students with varied opportunities to fashion their education into something that fits them, not the other way round. It also provides students an opportunity to finish a degree they might have started and were unable to continue with for one reason or another. The future of online degree education looks promising and opens up education to a larger section of the population than ever before.

EASIER TO FOCUS

It is not always easy to focus in class. Sometimes you're tired. Sometimes the person next to you smells like they need a shower. Sometimes there's construction going on right outside the classroom. Sometimes your study group wants to talk about something unrelated to school and sometimes your mind just wanders. It has been repeatedly shown that studying in a loud or noisy environment makes it much more difficult to concentrate.

With online classes, it's much easier to focus on what you're doing. Students can put themselves in the right environment. They can wear headphones if surroundings are noisy. Interactions happen online, meaning they won't easily wander off topic. The student can choose to study at a time when they are freshest. If students struggle to concentrate, online classes might be the ideal solution.

You Can Keep Your Job

Many times, getting a college degree requires quitting your job. After all, it can be difficult to juggle the demands of school and work simultaneously. But if you're organized and self-disciplined, it's often possible to do both. Because you don't have to attend class at a specific time, you can fulfill the functions of your job and study during your free time. Students can also use weekends to get additional work done that they did not have time for during the week. Juggling work and school is demanding; however, if students want to keep working while getting a degree, they can make it happen with online classes.

Learning New Tech Skills

For students who are not technology savvy, online classes will force them outside of their comfort zone, in a good way. Students will have to learn to navigate the course lectures, download materials, interact with others online and communicate well digitally. This may be scary for some students; however, as we are in the information age, these are essential skills and will allow students to keep pace with technology.

"You can't teach" people everything they need to know. The best you can do is position them where they can find what they need to know when they need to know it"

Seymour Paper, MIT mathematicians, educator, computer scientist

3

Challenges Students May Face with Online Learning

Online learning is not without some challenges, although it is this author's opinion that the benefits of online learning far outweigh the challenges. Some challenges with online learning include self-discipline and responsibility, critical thinking skills, technical skills, and lack of social interaction.

SELF-DISCIPLINE AND RESPONSIBILITY

Studying online requires more self-motivation and time-management skills because you will spend a lot of time on your own without your instructor physically close to keep you focused on deadlines. Instructors expect students to be independent, to learn on their own, and to engage with the material that they are teaching.

REFINED CRITICAL-THINKING SKILLS

Online learning facilitates the ability to think critically about what you do every day. The goal in the classroom is to challenge you to think differently, and you must be able to mater this skill. Critical thinking plays a role in any type of education; however, online learning forces you to develop your critical thinking skills in ways that you might not have practiced in an in-person classroom setting.

TECHNICAL SKILLS

Your online degree will require strong technical skills, a definite plus for any job seeker. As part of your coursework, you will likely need to utilize a learning management system and digitized learning materials and will need to get familiar with new tools and software and troubleshoot common issues. You will need to learn how to collaborate remotely with classmates in different time zones. You will need to learn how to use communication tools such as:

- Skype: This video conferencing software lets you speak face-to-face with your peers.

- Dropbox: Share documents with your group and keep work in one place using the file hosting service.

- Slack: This messaging platform is helpful if you need to instant message in real-time or break off into smaller groups to work on a specific part of the project.

- Trello or Basecamp: These project management tools enable you to and your team to create, assign, track, and prioritize to-dos.

LACK OF SOCIAL INTERACTION

Traditional students find that going to college is not just an intellectual activity, but it is also a social one. Students' interaction with their peers is greatly reduced in an online learning community. For the most part, students' complete online classes alone asynchronously, and any peer interaction happens on discussion boards and in chat rooms. Often, online classrooms can lack a sense of community. For some students, the lack of social interaction coupled with the need to be self-motivated to get their work done can lead to feelings of isolation.

SOME ONLINE COURSES CAN BE BORING

Although online training is meant to provide a solution to the boredom of classroom-based learning, this is not always the case. Many e-learning courses consist of never-ending texts followed by a long list of multiple choice questions that fail to engage students. More than e-learning, it feels like e-reading. If possible, students should look for online courses that are interactive, dynamic and fun, which are becoming more popular at education institutions.

"If you want to teach people a new way of thinking, don't bother trying to teach them. Instead, give them a tool, the use of which will lead to new ways of thinking"

R. Buckminster Fuller, author, inventor, architect, futurist

4

Determining If Online Learning Is for You

CHARACTERISTICS OF AN EFFECTIVE ONLINE LEARNER

Online learning is not for everyone and, generally, people who learn effectively in an online setting have the following characteristics:

Self-motivated and willing to accept responsibility for their own learning

You must have the ability to be an independent thinker. In an online program, you may not get direct instruction and student contact as in a traditional setting.

Self-disciplined, able to budget their time effectively and willing to stick to deadlines

You must have self-discipline to complete tasks on time. If you typically need reminders or other encouragements to get things done, you will need to commit to developing self-discipline and tools to manage your work.

Comfortable with technology, especially web-based and internet technologies

You must have some comfort in learning new technology as well as any of the technology required to take the class. Most programs require computer access with internet, word processing software, Adobe Acrobat and some video conferencing software, such as SKYPE. Skills necessary for many online courses include emailing, attaching and downloading documents, doing online research and communicating over Skype. If you do not already know how to do these things, you should be willing to learn.

Willing to accept the challenge of being an independent learner

In online classes, group discussions are not always possible online. You will need to be able to learn by reading and reviewing material on your own. Online classes do not have the same built-in accountability that comes from spending face-to-face time with a professor and fellow students. While you may be able to log in at times of your choosing, each course will also include deadlines for participation and assignment submission. You have to be aware of these dates and work steadily toward them.

Willing to take the initiative and contact their instructor when they have questions or concerns regarding the course

You will be able to call or email your instructor if you have difficulty with the directions or need feedback on assignments quickly; however, you may need patience and sometimes persistence to receive the clarification you need as most instructors' responses or comments are by emails or postings.

Ability to read, comprehend and communicate well in writing

One of the skill sets that are important for an online program is the ability to read and comprehend. There are ways to improve your reading ability if needed; you should consider this if reading and comprehension are a challenge for you.

Strategies for Staying Motivated to Complete the Online Learning Program

One of the biggest factors in online education success is being motivated to complete the program. Being motivated to reach an educational goal helps students stay on track. Online education requires self-discipline and personal drive. One key characteristic of people who succeed in online courses is that they drive themselves to achieve specific learning outcomes.

Although online courses are a perfect option for busy people with multiple demands on their time, the self-pacing aspect typically requires more initiative on the learner's part. Identified below are strategies for staying motivated enough to complete the program.

- **Reason** - Think about the reason you decided to return to school. Everyone's reason for embarking on an online program is different. Really, think about how the information you learn in the online program will move you forward to reaching your goal.

- **Goals** - Then create goals that are realistic, attainable goals to avoid the risk of disappointment. Start with smaller and achievable goals first, and as you obtain each goal it will serve as a catalyst to keep you motivated to keep going. When you set your goals, keep in mind to set a realistic and attainable schedule.

- **Schedule** - Start with a list of everything you have going on both personally and academically and create a schedule each month, how you plan to utilize your time. Do not fall to the "out of sight, out of mind" mindset as online courses let you set your own schedule. Remember to include in your schedule time for logging in to your learning management system on a regular basis. The goal is to aim for a balance in work, school and your online program. By creating and following a schedule, you will be less likely to let one of these areas overwhelm you.

- **Refreshment** - Make time to refresh and for personal enjoyment. Accomplishing a goal is great, but do not forget to do something nice for yourself. By both acknowledging and celebrating your small successes, you will create more motivation to keep moving.

- **Visualization** – Taking time to visualize your new life after finishing your online program will help keep you motivated. Look at the big picture and what your future will be like. Perhaps it will be a new career you love or a higher income; whatever the reason you are embarking on an online program, visualizing the positive outcomes can go a long way to relieving the feeling of struggling or being overwhelmed.

STUDENT ONLINE ASSESSMENT OF READINESS

Before enrolling in an online course, students should first assess their readiness for stepping into the online learning environment. Online learners need motivation and discipline to follow the weekly structure and stay current with course activities and assignments. Many students new to online learning have the false impression that online courses are "easier" than face-to-face courses. Strong online students are not "shy" about asking or answering questions, even challenging ones. They recognize that sharing questions and responses gives everyone the chance to explore course concepts in greater depth.

Learning through an online class requires different skills than learning in a face-to-face class. It's important to know what you're getting into and to understand the kind of commitment that's necessary for success in online learning. Most online learning assessments rate the following four characteristics, which are common in successful online students:

- Basic technical and academic skills
- Ability to study independently
- Good organizational skills
- Willing to devote the same amount of time and effort as a face-to-face course

Students can get a good idea of their readiness for online learning by filling out the following assessments.

ONLINE PROGRAM READINESS ASSESSMENT QUIZ 1

The following is an Online Program Readiness Assessment Quiz to help you discern if online learning is right for you. To find out, take the short quiz below. Be honest! No one will see the results but you.

1. I find classroom discussions are

  A. Always helpful

  B. Sometimes helpful

  C. Not helpful at all

2. Having face-to-face interaction with my instructor and other students is

  A. Very important to me

  B. Somewhat important to me

  C. Not particularly important to me

3. I need instructor feedback on assignments

  A. Right away or I may get frustrated

  B. Within a few days is fine

C. Within a week or two and I can review what I did

4. Typically I am a person who

A. Puts off things until the last minute

B. Requires reminders to get things done on time

C. Proactively gets things done ahead of time

5. When I get instructions for an assignment, I prefer

A. Having the instructor explain the assignment to me

B. Trying to follow directions on my own first

C. Figuring out the instructions by myself

6. The time I have to work on in an online course is

A. Less than the time I have for a classroom-based course

B. About the same time I have for a classroom-based course

C. More than the time I have for a classroom-based course

7. I would classify my reading ability as

A. Below average and require help interpreting what I read

B. Average, but I need some help to understand what is needed

C. Good. I usually understand what I read without much assistance

8. The hours I am available for classes are

A. Very flexible, and I can arrange my schedule easily

B. Somewhat flexible; I have commitments but am able to move things around if need be

C. Structure in that I am only available certain time each day

9. Having to go to a classroom on a regular basis for class is

A. Not difficult for me

B. Somewhat difficult but I can rearrange some priorities

C. Extremely difficult because of work and family obligations

10. When asked to try new software or computer programs

A. I get apprehensive, put it off or try to avoid it

B. I get apprehensive but try it anyway

C. I look forward to learning new technical skills

Now assign three points for every "C" answer, two points for every "B" answer and one point for every "A" answer. Add up your totals. If you scored 20 or above, it means that online courses are a good possibility for you. If you scored less than 20, it means that there are some challenges you may have with entering online programs; however, by recognizing those challenges now you will have a better chance of overcoming them.

ONLINE PROGRAM READINESS ASSESSMENT QUIZ 2

Instructions: For each row in the table below, choose the "☐" that best describes you. When you are finished, read the guidelines for interpreting the score

I am comfortable and proficient at creating, saving, locating, and opening different types of files on a computer.	☐ 1 ☐	I am not comfortable or proficient working with files on a computer.
I have reliable access to a high-speed Internet connection (DSL, cable, dorm, etc)	☐ 2 ☐	I have regular access only to a dial-up modem for Internet access.
I know how to check my official school.edu email account and I can access it regularly to check for new messages.	☐ 1 ☐	I have never checked my official school.edu email account.

Determining If Online Learning Is for You

| I have access to a webcam and microphone for simple multimedia participation. | ☐ 2 ☐ | I do not have a webcam and microphone, or I will need to borrow those things. |

| I have no problem retaining information if I read it. | ☐ 2 ☐ | I retain information better if I hear it spoken directly to me. |

| I am comfortable using online discussion forums. | ☐ 1 ☐ | I have never really posted messages to an online forum before. |

| I am usually able to stay on task and avoid distractions (texting, Facebook) while studying. | ☐ 3 ☐ | I get distracted easily while studying and need a lot of time to accomplish my work. |

| I am very good at planning and managing my time so that my work is on time and complete. | ☐ 4 ☐ | I am ok with time management but have had to ask professors for extensions in the past. |

Setting aside a regular 5-8 hours per week to devote to an online class is possible for me.	☐ 3 ☐	It's hard for me to predict when I'll be able to do the online work. Besides, I thought you could do the work whenever you wanted...right?
I have little or no trouble expressing myself in writing using formal grammar and spelling.	☐ 3 ☐	I have found using formal grammar and spelling to be a challenge in expressing myself.
I am comfortable learning through individual reading and study.	☐ 3 ☐	I usually need direct explanation by an instructor and face-to-face interaction with peers to feel comfortable learning material.

I can learn from a variety of formats (lectures, videos, podcasts, online discussion/ conferencing).	☐ 2 ☐	My learning style usually requires a structured lecture at its core.
I know how to login to Blackboard and I am familiar with using the most common tools.	☐ 1 ☐	I have little or no experience accessing and using Blackboard.
I have my own relatively new computer (2-3 years old) onto which I can install any additional software necessary for the course.	☐ 3 ☐	My computer is 5-7 years old. —or— I use the computer labs on campus or someone else's to do my work.

| If I can't figure out something, I am comfortable asking my classmates or the instructor for help via email, discussion board, or chat. | ☐ 4 ☐ | Meeting with my professor in person to ask questions is more comfortable for me. |

| Online is good choice | ⇐ Total ⇒ | Online may not be a good choice |

INTERPRETING THE RESULTS

A total score of **17** or higher in *the right-hand column* is a strong indication that you will likely face more challenges than may be desired in an online class. While online may not be the best choice at the moment, if you are still interested in being an online student, you should understand some of the challenges and what you need to do to overcome them.

Questions that are weigh ted "3" and "4" in the center column address crucial study skills needed for an online class. The most successful online students will have answered all of those questions in the left-hand column (regardless of what their total score happens to be) or will work to address them over the course of the semester.

Questions weighted "1" and "2" are also important for an online class, but many of the topics they address are things that don't automatically block a student's academic success in the class or can be remedied once the class begins.

This work is licensed under a Creative Commons Attribution-NonCommercial-ShareAlike 4.0 International License. Glenn Pillsbury at Stanislaus State and published freely under a Creative Commons Attribution 4.0 license at https://www.csustan.edu/teach-online/online-readiness-self-assessment.

"An investment in knowledge always pays the best interest"

Benjamin Franklin

5

Choosing an Online Learning Program

Chapter 4 discussed how to determine if online learning is right for the student. Chapter 5 details further considerations students will need after the student has made the decision to move forward with an online degree program. Removing the constraints of time and distance, studying online opens up countless options and opportunities, but without the classic road trip to get the feel of an institution, how should a student know which college to choose? Finding the right college to fit your needs requires some savvy online searching. Before students put their career on the line, it is essential that they choose a high-quality online degree program that is committed to their educational success. If students choose a subpar program, they may find themselves floundering with little direction and on the fast track to high student debt. Fortunately, there are many excellent degree programs available 100% online that can help students affordably achieve their academic goals and find career success.

Managing Online Education Expectations

Every student has some expectations of what college life will entail; however, having unrealistic expectations can lead to disappointment. Students have expectations of their degree courses, thus they may take the course with the preconceived notion that they will enjoy its every phase or that it will be a revelation in terms of its instruction or course content. However, most will end up being disappointed on that front because there is nothing very inspiring about a degree. It only involves hard work and dedication on the part of the student. The disillusion is more pronounced in those students taking an online degree course because they have to struggle much more compared to a student opting for a normal degree course. However, the long-term benefits of completing any educational qualification will fulfill the students' expectations.

Expectations as regards the manageability of the course content run incredibly high. The work involved for an online degree is the same as that required for a normal degree course. However, most online degrees are difficult to manage as the students are expected to study on their own without guidance and instruction from a teacher or lecturer. A great deal of self-discipline is required to manage an online education while simultaneously working or looking after a family. Time management is of the utmost importance and in such circumstances most students find it difficult to cope with the stress and burdens of an online degree.

To give an idea of what exactly is involved in an online degree and to help manage expectations, students can read the accounts of other students who have gone through the experience. Students will find a number of their peers will speak about online programs in glowing terms, while there are many others who will be quite candid in expressing their inability to cope with the workload or the lack of time to meet the deadlines or the problems they faced due to an unsupportive employer. There may be some resentment if you take up a degree course while you are employed, though this may not be an issue if you are taking the course for further advancement in your present job. If students prepare to take this resentment in their stride, then it will not be much of a bother, and if there is no resentment, then so much the better!

The best way to manage your own expectations is to approach the issue with an open mind and not expect anything from it. Managing to complete an online degree course along with personal commitments like looking after a family or going to a job every day is a difficult task. It takes a lot of effort, but if you expect it to be difficult and yet achieve your goal, then it will give you tremendous satisfaction and a sense of achievement. If you expect the worst, maybe you will be pleasantly surprised!

ENSURING A QUALITY EDUCATION

This book would be remiss if it did not cover how students can ensure they are attending a quality online school and online program. Clearly online programs cannot provide many of the informal social interactions students have at school, but how online courses will do in terms of moving students' learning forward requires students to do their own research to find the best school and program for them. To conduct thorough research, students should consider these key questions to ask to ensure they are investing their time in a quality program.

How long has the online college been around?

Many online degree programs are offered by colleges and universities that have been around for decades. Earning a degree online from a school with an established reputation, the degree already has a perception of proven value. Choosing to attend a school with shorter institutional history will require students to review the school's relationships and partnerships within the educational community, institutions, employers, and alumni. Students should look at the education institution's success in the program being considered as well as students' satisfaction rates. Students should also pay some attention to public opinion and particularly employers' perceptions. If students are aware of an employer in their field, they should ask what the employer thinks about the merits of the schools they are considering.

Is the college or university accredited?

There is a wide variety of guidelines that students should bear in mind to make sure that they are on the right track. In the United States of America, accreditation usually involves governmental agencies and non-governmental entities. Accreditation is a quality measure that students should consider to protect the value of their education.

The ultimate mission of an accreditation organization is to help those online schools to get hold of positive student learning outcomes. Students who prefer to enroll in online schools should also be aware that accreditation doesn't guarantee the success of a certain student. It is up to the student to make the most out of the education that online schools offer them.

However, if most of the students who enrolled at online schools are unsuccessful or don't demonstrate high levels of educational performance, this is the right time for an accreditation organization to step in and examine the effectiveness of online schools and at the same time evaluate the aspects that can be enhanced.

According to the U.S. Department of Education, the goal of accreditation is to ensure that the education provided by institutions of higher education meets acceptable levels of quality. To avoid having credentials questioned or even transferring credits to other institutions, students should not invest money in a school that is not accredited by the appropriate agencies. Accrediting agencies are recognized as private educational associations of a national scope wherein they are the ones that develop the evaluation criteria and at the same time conduct peer evaluations to easily and quickly assess if the criteria are successfully met. Without the seal of approval, that piece of bond paper that students will get after their graduation is worth less than one from an accredited education institution. How can students tell if a certain online school is reputable or not? This is one of the most common questions that people want to know the answer to.

The first thing you need to do is ask the school if they are accredited. Reputable online schools will not find it hard to tell you if they are truly accredited. Furthermore, reputable online schools will tell you the state they are accredited in and which educational governing bodies have accredited them. If you really want to make sure, you can personally check the institution that accredited them.

In order for you to know if the online school that you opt into is a reputable one it's best to be wary of life-experience courses. One of the most common warning signs of a bad online school is if they claim to provide an accredited life-experience degree without any examinations and classes. These could be an MBA or BA. Don't be fooled by these kinds of online schools. You need to be aware that there is no such thing as an accredited degree that is purely based on life experiences.

The next thing you need to do is to check the accreditation agencies that they mention to you. By doing this, students can easily determine if the online school that they chose is a reputable one. Don't waste money, time and effort for those non-accredited online schools that are being offered online.

Not all accreditation is the same, and it's important to understand the differences. Colleges can be accredited on regional, national and specialized levels.

Regional accreditation is governed by the home state and recognized nationally by the Council for Higher Education Accreditation. Colorado State University is accredited by the Higher Learning Commission, which grants membership to schools across the North Central region. The standards for this accreditation are particularly high, requiring general education courses and only accepting transfer credits from equally accredited colleges.

National accreditation is usually sought by specific types of schools that don't necessarily adhere to traditional teaching practices. It is used for alternative colleges, such as trade schools, some distance learning bodies, and religious schools. Specialized accreditation is used for specific programs, accredited by agencies that do not accredit entire learning institutions.

Some online schools opt for national or specialized accreditation, but this accreditation is not as universally recognized as regional accreditation. This can create issues in transferring credits between institutions. Be sure to fully investigate a school's accreditation, especially if you think you may someday transfer schools, to avoid end up investing time and money in courses that cannot be transferred.

Students who research the database of the Department of Education can easily find in-depth details and information on national and regional accrediting agencies that are recognized by higher education. Bear in mind that not all online schools are accredited and this is one of the main reasons why you need to ensure that your chosen degree programs are accredited.

DOES THE ONLINE DEGREE PROGRAM ACCEPT TRANSFER CREDITS?

According to research, one of the best ways to reduce taking on student debt and increase your chances of graduating on time is to enroll exclusively in courses that offer a direct route to graduation. Online degree programs that make it easy to transfer existing college credits or low-cost online courses are most likely to offer a direct pathway to your degree.

At many schools, the transfer policy is the same for online programs as with traditional on-campus programs. Typically, how many credits will transfer will be determined on a case-by-case basis. For many students, their new school will examine their transcript and look at each credit and course to make a determination if courses will transfer and, if so, how many credits will transfer. The new school may need more than just a course title to make this determination. It may also need a course description and copies of course materials, such as the syllabus and list of textbooks.

Is the school in a good financial position?

Use caution when considering schools that are experiencing financial challenges, are reluctant to share important financial data, or have seemed to just set up shop without prior academic success or experience. Look to see if they have strong ties or relationships with partners and respected academic institutions.

There are ways to check the financial health of a college including asking the following:

WHAT PHYSICAL SHAPE IS THE SCHOOL IN?

Institutions with cash flow problems often put off millions of dollars of maintenance and it shows. As you look at the virtual campus, you will probably get a feel within the first few minutes of what the campus is like. See if there is evidence of disrepair, if buildings appear well cared for and if they're technologically up to date. These things shine light on whether an institution has the resources needed to keep its facilities in good operating order. The more you see that concerns you the more you should wonder if a school has enough money to provide a quality educational experience.

HOW BIG IS THE ENDOWMENT?

When it comes to a college or university's endowment, size matters. An endowment is a permanent fund that universities and their foundations use to collect and invest funds given by philanthropic donors. Most schools use interest and dividends earned from the funds in their endowment to pay for various things, such as student aid programs and financial support for study abroad and internships.

You can find out what the institution's endowment is through an online search. Generally speaking, the larger the endowment the better able an institution is to finance its operations and the stabler it is for the long run. At the time this book is being written, only 106 institutions have endowments of more than US$1 billion. But the size of the endowment isn't the only thing to consider. To preserve the value of the endowment spending for both current and future students, historically, colleges were advised to spend only about 5% of their endowments each year. Institutions that spend above that amount over a longer period of time can potentially erode the value of their endowments, unless they attract more donations or gain other sources of revenue. For that reason, institutions that spend more than 5% assume larger risks for the future market value of the endowment.

An endowment spending rate of more than 5% may be also a sign of budget stress and another potential red flag. There is no single place that you can go to find out the spending rate of the endowment. Some institutions, such as Elon and Yale, publish this information on their websites, but many do not. Often, the only way to find out is to ask. Students might start by asking the director of admissions or chief financial officer.

WHAT IS THE TUITION DISCOUNT RATE?

At private colleges, student should ask, "What is the school's tuition discount rate?" These discounts are actually tuition dollars that families or students pay that are redistributed for very good reasons to support students with high financial need or to attract students with special talents. Learning environments that are diverse and vibrant benefit all students. This tuition money gets redistributed in the form of need-based financial awards, merit financial awards and athletic financial awards.

According to the National Association of College and University Business Officers, the average tuition discount rate for incoming freshmen in 2018–19 was **52.2%**. When an institution is using 52% of every dollar they take in for discounting, that leaves only 48% for everything else, such as faculty and staff salaries, student support services, facilities and utilities. A tuition discount rate higher than the average rate can be a sign of trouble.

If you have never understood why the sticker price of college is not what you end up paying, a big part of that answer for private colleges is the tuition discount rate.

CHECK DATABASES

Check out federal databases to get key measures about a school's performance. The College Scorecard located at https://collegescorecard.ed.gov, for instance, is a free U.S. Department of Education site that provides information on a variety of measures, including the size of the student body, cost, graduation rates and how much students are expected to earn after they graduate.

The education department also publishes a Financial Responsibility Composite Score for each institution in the U.S. that receives federal aid located at https://studentaid.gov/data-center/school/composite-scores. This score rates each school's ability to meet the standards of financial responsibility necessary to participate in federal financial aid programs. The range of scores is a high of 3 to a low of -1. While this simple score might not tell the complete story of a school, it is a key indicator of whether a school is in good financial health.

SEARCH ONLINE

Get online and broadly research institutions students are considering. Many state university systems are considering mergers because of declining enrollment. Students' research will also help them uncover potential trouble spots: Is the school's accreditation threatened? Has enrollment been on the decline? Has there been frequent turnover in leadership? None of these things are good for a college or university in the future.

At the time of wring this book, there are more than 4,500 colleges and universities in the U.S. Most of them can make a major difference in a student's life. But some are in danger or closing. Before investing your money by paying your own costs or footing the bill for a loved one to attend a particular college, understand that the responsibility for doing research and asking questions is yours.

ARE THERE ANY HIDDEN COSTS?

Sometimes there can be hidden costs to an online degree program, from technology to lab fees. Reputable programs will make sure any "extra" costs are transparent, such as if there are any on-campus requirements. Also, be sure to explore the financial consequences of taking any time off. An advantage of taking your general education course online, prior to enrolling in an online degree program, is that you can take as many courses as you want and work at your own pace.

WHAT IS THE COST AND AVERAGE STUDENT DEBT?

There is an enormous variation in the cost of online degree programs. There are many excellent, high-quality, flexible and reputable online degree programs that can help students affordably earn their college degree. Be aware that just because students can pay for their degree program with the help of loans does not make the degree program affordable. Students have to be able to pay their student loan debt back without sacrificing their future. Therefore, the key to choosing an affordable degree program is focusing on lowering your tuition costs.

For example, one year of tuition and fees at a four-year private college is $30,094, but online programs offering competency-based degrees only cost between $2,500 and $6,000 per year. Alternatively, students who take advantage of scholarships and tuition discounts available through an online course provider like StraighterLine can save up to 60% on the total cost of their degree through a network of accredited colleges.

With online courses and online degree programs, students have an extraordinary opportunity to graduate with the degree they want, from the school they want for a fraction of the price. Students should know their options, ask the right questions—and be confident that they can find an online college that's right for them.

Financial aid options are also particularly important. Studying online should be flexible, so find a college whose costs and payment plans suit you. Students should be able to have a pressure-free discussion about payment and financial aid options with a school's financial aid advisors. If it isn't easy to do, this should raise a red flag. Be wary of schools that don't have your best financial and academic interests in mind.

CAN THE DEGREE PROGRAM HELP YOU REACH YOUR CAREER GOALS?

Too many students load up on excessive and unnecessary credits and end up spending too much time and money to complete their degrees. Make sure the courses and degree make sense for your post-graduation goals. Students are advised to look for, and review, a degree plan before they enroll. Students should verify student employment and placement rates and understand the value of their degree to potential employers.

Paying for college is a massive commitment, but it's important to look beyond the up-front fees. Consider the overarching value of your degree. Will it directly lead to a job in a specific industry? Will it give marketable skills that will give you a competitive edge in your job search? Will it lead to a personally fulfilling career? The value of a degree can be measured by a number of different personal priorities.

Ask what the college can offer in terms of professional ongoing support after graduation. Students want to ensure their online degree program will help them enter into, or advance in, their chosen career field. Does the school offer career services? Is there an alumni association that hosts networking events? Are faculty members connected to employers in your field? Is the school supporting you not only in educational achievement but when you want to get that next job?

ARE THE ONLINE COURSES BEST IN CLASS?

Not all online courses are made equal. Courses with stale material can put students out of step in a changing workplace. Check which textbooks are required, if they are reputable and up to date. Find out if taking lab courses online and at home is possible. Also, many of the best online programs will use a solid learning management system so students will benefit from the latest learning content and technologies and enjoy greater success.

WHAT TYPE OF ACADEMIC, CAREER, AND TECHNICAL SUPPORT IS AVAILABLE TO ONLINE STUDENTS?

Earning a degree online doesn't eliminate the need for academic assistance. In fact, in most cases, it increases the need for those services. Students need to know what level of support they will have. Who is going to help students day one, week one, when they need help?

A well-staffed support team can help you get the academic support you need, when you need it, as well as help keep you on track for an on-time graduation. Check out online tutoring options and access to student advisors. Don't base your decision on a program's sale pitch without ensuring that online students have equal access to available career service support and opportunities.

Also, as an online student, you can expect to encounter technical issues from time to time. Be sure the online degree program you are considering has multiple methods for you to walk through any technology-based issues, including chat, phone, or email.

The online learning experience may be technically challenging, so, to avoid being isolated, students should find out what options the college offers in regards to speaking with advisors and other students. Also, students should look at how classes are conducted and whether there are opportunities to interact with peers on a regular basis. A community of support and interaction is important when studying online.

By asking those hard questions, online students can also get a feel for how responsive a school is to their needs. If information about support services is not readily available on a school's website, or if students have a hard time getting answers when they call, the program may be trying to hide something. If you're having a hard time getting information about what it would be like as a student at that school, that is going to tell you a lot about what your experience would be. If you can't get a hold of anyone to ask about their academic counseling or career placement services, that may be red flag.

"If everybody participates at the deadline, the quality of the conversation is very, very surface level and doesn't delve anywhere close to where it should be for a thoughtful and informative discussion"

Brian Redmond, Professor, Pennsylvania State University

6

Discussion Boards

A common myth about online learning is that online students are isolated and can remain anonymous and that online learning lacks the lively scholarly debate that takes place in a traditional on-ground classroom. That myth is totally busted. Unlike traditional students in campus-based classes, online students cannot hide at the back of a massive lecture hall. All online students are required to participate by interacting with each other and with the instructor. That interaction occurs through online discussion boards.

WHAT IS A DISCUSSION BOARD POST?

In an online class, discussion posts are the main way students and professors interact with the course lessons and curriculum. The best discussion posts demonstrate an understanding of the course material and present a cohesive argument with evidence to support the argument. In online classes, discussion boards give students the opportunity to talk about course topics with each other, and with the professor, similar to how they would if they were in a traditional classroom. This helps students absorb the class material and share ideas.

Discussion questions are designed to probe further into some aspects of the weekly course content, which could be through a current event, a recent court ruling, or a related hot-button topic. It is an opportunity for students to make a personal examination of what the weekly topic means to them and gives every member of the class the opportunity to express an opinion and be heard.

While specific requirements may vary depending on the course and the instructor, basic requirements generally include a weekly discussion question or a choice of multiple weekly questions, to which students are required to make an initial post by mid-week. After that, students usually respond to at least one or two posts from others in the class or to additional questions from the instructor before the end of the week.

Because discussion posts are graded and contribute to a student's success in the course, it is important for online students to learn how to develop strong posts that add to a meaningful learning experience. In fact, the advantage of an online discussion forum over a classroom discussion is that you have the time to carefully craft your responses without feeling rushed. Taking your time and working carefully is important to crafting a quality post.

Discussion boards have been a staple of online courses for decades and instructors often ask students to respond to an assigned reading and their peers. However, to prevent plagiarism, some learning management systems are set up, either by the platform or by policies of the institution or instructor, to only reveal the full contents of a discussion thread after a student has already posted. In the classroom, students and professors hold discussions about the subject matter. Discussion posts duplicate this interaction when you are online. In the virtual classroom, you use the keyboard instead of your voice.

When posting, students are advised to keep their tone and language conversational. It is also generally a good idea to respond to other people's postings and really do your part to facilitate a real conversation. Before writing a single word, make sure you have prepared by doing any coursework, required reading, assignments, research, etc. No one wants to read a post that rambles on and does not have a point. Whether you are a seasoned online student or are taking your very first online class, online discussion posts are central to your online learning experience.

As a portion of the student's grade will be based on discussion board participation including the quality of their postings, it is essential for online students to be aware of strategies for creating a solid discussion board posting that demonstrates their command of the material and engagement with their fellow classmates.

While weekly discussion posts can be a bit intimidating at first, they are an opportunity to practice your academic writing skills and to hone your ability to craft, present, and defend your reasoned responses relying on logic and facts. Simply keep in mind that there really is no 'right' position. What is vital is that you learn how to defend whatever your position is. Students who are brand new to online learning could easily approach their first discussion post assignment with some uneasiness, but if they treat it like a discussion occurring in class, they will get better at postings in time.

Just as traditional students should follow certain etiquette in the classroom, online students engaging in discussions on a board are expected to behave appropriately. The following are some strategies, guidelines and tips to help students create posts and responses so they do well in their online courses while following standards that professors expect.

Strategies and Tips for Discussion Board Postings

Complete the Assigned Reading First

It may sound obvious but, first and foremost, students should complete their homework or assigned readings before writing their post. As the student reads, they should make connections between the text and their own personal experience. The student should try to become immersed in the readings so when they are ready to begin writing, they will be fully prepared to present an authentic, meaningful response. Also, you should be sure to take a look at your instructor's feedback on previous assignments to make sure you follow all expectations.

Look very carefully at the posting criteria

Students should consider what question or required reading they are being asked to respond to. They need to consider requirements such as the word limit, specific formatting, due date, time the project is due (in their time zone), and the sources of information they are to draw the information from. Sometimes instructors may ask the student to reflect on personal experiences, determine a solution to a problem, compare two ideas, or make an argument. The instructor will provide the student with the grading criteria on how their discussion post will be evaluated.

Read the discussion posting directions carefully

Before starting to write the discussion board, students should evaluate what they're being asked to comment on to make sure they know what they are supposed to write about. Sometimes it is a personal response, sometimes it is a chance to absorb the material by restating the ideas presented in the reading, and sometimes the discussion board is a combination of ideas. It is also a good idea to read all the related discussion questions and points being asked to comment on before starting the reading and other assignments. That way the topic will be on your mind when you are studying.

Follow the rules of discussion postings

If the student is asked to write a response to a question and respond to other postings, they will need to make sure they comply with this request. To select the best posting to respond to, think about the classroom environment. Look at the post and determine whether you would respond if somebody said that in class. If so, respond to the post. If not, move on to the next posting.

Most courses have rules for discussions in the syllabus or course introduction such as how many times the student is required to post as well as guidelines for responding to their peers. Students should make sure to read and understand these rules before writing that first post.

Include adequate detail in your postings

Students should not ever write only, "I agree," or, "Good idea," or any other short response to another posting. Rather they must be sure to include details. For example, a response of, "I agree with David," is not enough. It is better to write, "I agree with David. I had a similar experience where Theory XYZ came into play…" and the second discussion board will get you a much better grade than the first. Also, remember that it is fine to disagree with a classmate's posting, but respond in a respectful and polite way if you disagree and make sure you explain why.

START WITH A STRONG ARGUMENT

When composing your discussion board, one strategy is to start a strong argument and then support statements with evidence from the course materials. Students may have to do external research and be sure to cite correctly, but they should try to be concise and articulate their ideas thoroughly. Explore all parts of the discussion question and try to get other students to think beyond the obvious. Think about what you want to say to your fellow classmates and your professor and try to limit yourself to the topic, making sure any points you make are relevant. An "A+" posting will make that connection between the theories and ideas and real life.

(Hint: You can always email your professor for clarification if you don't understand something, just do it early enough to get the post in on time)

INCLUDE PERSONAL OR PROFESSIONAL EXPERIENCE

Include personal or professional experience (when it is applicable) and support your ideas with textual evidence. Offer real-world application of these ideas to bring added value to the conversation as this may resonate with other students. Remember to always relate direct references to concepts you are learning about and establish those connections with evidence from academic sources. Try doing something extra that requires others to think and respond to the ideas you are sharing. Use topic sentences to bring all points together and dig deep to find connections beyond the surface. Be sure that you have proposed a unique perspective that can be challenged by your classmates. Sometimes a quick story makes a better point than a long ramble about the theory. Applying the class information to real life is what discussions are usually about to make a connection between real life and the information.

Prepare your response in a text editor like (MS Word) before you post

In doing so, you will have a better chance to ensure the post is cohesive, coherent, and complete. Make sure to check all spelling and grammar. When writing the actual post, be sure to use the tools in your course management system to write your response. Use bullets and paragraphs to format the text; if available, use the preview tool and especially make use of the spell checker. After using your favorite word-processing software or text editor to make sure the postings are grammatically correct and error free, copy and paste (<Ctrl-C> and <Ctrl-V>) your posting to the discussion board.

ENGAGE WITH YOUR CLASSMATES

Post your response, engage with your classmates, and continue to ask follow-up questions. Be an integral part of the conversation and add value to what is being discussed. Some of the best online discussions continue in the minds of others long after you have posted to the discussion forum. The next time you post, ask yourself, "What can I write that will add value to the conversation?"

A discussion board is not just a place where you are checking off a course requirement. It is a place where you can get to know your fellow classmates as well as your professor. It is also your opportunity to share information with others and, most importantly, to get help.

GATHER SUPPORTING FACTS AND POINTS OF VIEW

Any strong point must also have backup documentation. That backup can come in many forms including the course material, the news, research studies or even your own personal experiences. Including these points in posts will also demonstrate knowledge and understanding of the topic. It is a good idea to have these points jotted off to the side and handy so when writing your posts these points do not break your train of thought.

For any reference that you do make in your post, be sure to cite it properly. Even if it is a discussion posting, not giving others credit for their work is plagiarism. Your citation does not have to be formal unless stated in the syllabus. Just make sure others can find the information from the citation by giving the title, author, and date. Students can take a look at BibMe.org or OttoBib.com to help automate their formal citations. References from verifiable supporting information such as vetted websites, reliable academic e-books, and reports of research from the Scholarly Literature journal also help forum members better answer your questions as they can clearly reflect your point of view.

Be serious about the assignment

Students should take discussion boards assignments seriously as it is a way to demonstrate that they have digested the assigned reading and are thinking about it in a way that will allow them to apply the knowledge in practice. They should avoid making jokes. When posting on the internet, it can be difficult to know when someone is joking because readers cannot see the person's nonverbal communication.

Discussion Boards

Online discussion boards are no exception to this issue. To avoid confusion and risk of offending others in the class, it is best to avoid jokes and sarcasm when posting. Students should avoid language that is not appropriate for an academic setting.

Use simple formatting and post with clarity

When it comes to formatting, students should keep it as simple as possible by avoiding fonts that are difficult to read. This ensures that everyone can easily read the points being made and keep the discussion flowing. Students should express themselves as clearly as possible. That means using correct grammar to the best of your ability, avoiding acronyms and slang, and proofreading your writing, possibly referring to dictionaries and grammar sources.

Post on time!

Nothing is worse for a professor than reading through a lively set of discussion posts and finding the late ones at the bottom. It's like coming up to the professor after class to contribute your information. Remember, the early bird gets the worm (both on and offline)! If you are asked to post to a question and then respond to others, do the first posting early and the responses towards the end of the time allotted for the assignment. You will be noticed if you start a good discussion.

Common Online Discussion Board Pitfalls and How to Avoid Them

Students who are not used to online courses are likely to make some mistakes when they participate in a discussion board. Students' discussions are related to what they are learning and reading about in their course. So, even if it is not explicitly stated, they are expected to use concepts and ideas from their weekly reading in their discussion board post. The following are some mistakes that students should be aware of in order to avoid them.

Not being thorough

Many students simply do not address the writing prompt thoroughly in their post. Sometimes a prompt will require that a student addresses two to three points, but students may fail to do so. Sometimes, responses are written in a way that does not reflect that they have read the original post well. The response does not continue the discussion. Responses often appear rushed and unplanned. Students should put effort into their posts and responses in a way that adds to the learning of both them and their classmates. Give thorough

Discussion Boards

consideration to classmates' postings and respond constructively with something substantive.

MAKING POSTS TOO LONG

Unless there is a word count required by the instructor, try to develop shorter posts, much shorter than a screen-worth of information. Please be polite and supportive, commenting and connecting the ideas of others into new learning for oneself and the community.

PROCRASTINATION

Waiting until the last minute to make a required post can decrease the quality of the conversation about a subject. Posting earlier allows other students to respond to a post and engage in debates that help everyone in the class get the most out of the conversation. Students need to be proactive when digesting new material each week. Remember, if you don't understand something, email your instructor right away and ask for clarification.

NOT PAYING ATTENTION

One mistake students make is not doing the reading or assignment in advance. Another mistake is not reading other students' posts and responding to points already made.

Instead, many students repeat points already made without acknowledging that they are repeating the same ideas. As a result, they do not get full credit for their discussion board posting.

Discussion Board Student Checklist.

The following are a list of questions that students should ask before posting their discussion board to help ensure they will receive a good grade.

- ✓ Did you carefully read the discussion instructions and understand the purpose of the question?
- ✓ Did you think about how this post is related to what you are learning about in your course?
- ✓ Did you complete all required reading and identify all the key terms in the reading?
- ✓ Did you note any additional requirements such as word count or citation formatting?
- ✓ Did you review the grading rubric (if provided)?
- ✓ Does your post contain a fully developed paragraph for each of the questions or action words in the discussion instructions?

- ✓ Did you include concepts, ideas, or information from the course readings in your post wherever possible?

- ✓ Did you correctly cite your sources as you used them?

- ✓ Did you review your writing for correct grammar, punctuation, and spelling?

- ✓ Did you offer personal observations and knowledge in an accurate and insightful way?

"The students of the future will demand the learning support that is appropriate for their situation or context. Nothing more, nothing less. And they want it at the moment the need arises. Not sooner, not later. Mobile devices will be a key technology to provide that learning support"

Dr. Marcus Specht, Professor of Advanced Learning Technologies, Open University of the Netherlands

7

Learning Management Systems

WHAT ARE LEARNING MANAGEMENT SYSTEMS?

College and university online courses take place in a cloud-based environment where students can attend virtually anywhere. The school must have a dedicated environment or platform where students can go to access course materials, participate in class discussions, and submit materials for grading. These platforms are mostly known as learning management systems or LMS.

The LMS is designed to fulfill all aspects of the online learning process, from administering course materials and assignments to documenting class participation and grades. The LMS provides the structure into which online instructors deliver course content. While learning management systems are essential for making modern distance learning courses possible, they are now widely used in traditional college courses as well. However, with the increasing popularity of online learning, coupled with not every online college student being tech savvy, schools are required to make online college courses accessible to students who do not have a technical background. Therefore, one of the most important aspects of a learning management system is that it must be easy for students to understand and use, regardless of the individual students' level of technical and computer expertise. Most LMS programs are "intuitive," avoiding students having to spend a lot of time learning how to use the LMS system and instead they can focus their efforts on learning the course material. Students should think of their learning management system as a virtual classroom.

Universities and colleges use a host of different types of learning management systems each with a unique set of features to meet the specific requirements of course curricula. However, all learning management systems have several functions in common such as course creation, assessment, grading, multi-device access and interactive resources.

Universities and colleges use learning management systems to streamline the education process, making it easier and quicker for the instructor with self-marking quizzes and tests while keeping all student results in one place.

Technology has the potential to engage and motivate learners more than ever before and with an intuitive learning management system, so students may see interaction and subsequently results improve. In particular, features that motivate students, improve their achievement and make learning more enjoyable result in learning management systems actually encouraging interaction between learners and educators. More engagement can benefit both the student and the instructor and lead to a better quality of education and higher results.

WHAT IS THE PRIMARY FUNCTION OF THE LMS?

The role of a Learning Management System varies depending on the college or university objectives, online training curriculum, and desired outcomes. However, the most common use for LMS software is to deploy and track online training. Typically, curricula are uploaded to the Learning Management System, which makes them easily accessible for remote learners.

Therefore students should think of their Learning Management System as a vast repository where their instructor can store and track information. Anyone with a login and password can access these online training resources whenever and wherever. For schools using a local rather than a cloud-based learning management system, students will be provided with several options to access their learning management system. With a self-hosted learning management system, users must also have the LMS software installed on their hard drive or access to the school's server. For desktop application the LMS is installed on the desktop, usually through an app, and is accessible on multiple devices, making it easy for the students to collaborate with other students and/or the instructor. For Mobile application, learning management systems are accessible whenever, wherever via mobile devices. Students can upload their work and track online training progress on the go. Whatever the installation option, the thing to bear in mind is that LMS users fall into two categories: First, online learners who use the Learning Management System to participate in online training courses; second, the instructor who relies on the LMS platform to dispense information and update the online training content for the students.

FEATURES OF LEARNING MANAGEMENTS SYSTEMS

Course creation is one of the primary functions of an LMS. Instructors can create custom courses and keep them private or public and enable access anytime or anywhere. LMS systems allow for developing online content and support training using docs, videos, presentations, tests, exams, and quizzes.

Learning management systems are used for ongoing assessment of the students' learning. LMSs help learners know how much information they have retained after going through the entire course but can be a motivator for students to perform better in their future. Instructors can keep track of real-time learning activities of the students and provide feedback on the same with the help of an LMS.

Grading the overall performance and each assessment result is a major use for the LMS. The LMS provides students with grades and scores, which allows them to get to know which areas are in need of improvement. Most LMSs offer a communication avenue to their instructor or other peers. With user-generated content sharing knowledge and experiences with other students becomes easy. Learners can clarify doubts and solve problems together through active learning. If learners feel confused or have queries while going through their courses, they can take suggestions from their peers and clear their doubts. Instructors can also exchange ideas and views among themselves on any topic based on their personal experiences.

Many web-based LMSs provide multiple device access, which means students can take their courses anytime, anywhere on any device such as a smartphone, desktop or tablet. This convenient feature can deliver a better learning experience to the student.

Finally, LMS systems allow instructors to be able to incorporate multimedia into their online courses to engage their students as well as to promote better knowledge retention. You may use multimedia in different forms such as audio, video, GIFs, and so on. Gamification is a key feature that introduces game elements in learning and keeps students motivated and engaged with their courses by using rewards, points, badges, and certificates. These interactive resources not only make a course engaging but also help in ensuring a better retention capacity in multiple types of learners.

Depending on the LMS the educational institution uses, there are select premier functions that instructors are able to perform such as analytics to track learning activities and performance of each learner or group of learners and document management, which allows instructors to reuse similar training programs for multiple courses.

TYPES OF LEARNING MANAGEMENT SYSTEMS

There are many types of learning management systems, but this book will provide a summary of the leading four in order of popularity—Blackboard Collaborate, Moodle, Schoology and Canvas.

One of the most popular LMS choices in the education segment, Blackboard comes as software as a service (SaaS) model and a non-SaaS model, which allows educators to deliver assessments and track grades, along with the ability to manage both blended and online classes. Blackboard Collaborate also allows the student to connect to commercial content through some major publishers and journals. For the instructor Blackboard Collaborate allows the intelligence needed to track retention, enrollment, and engagement. The Blackboard platform operates as well as a desktop. In addition to its functionality, Blackboard's integration with Collaborate, an online web conferencing system, enables students to attend class anywhere virtually.

Moodle is one of the most popular learning management systems around; Moodle has a solid functionality and offers everything a higher education institution will need to service its students. One of the benefits of Moodle for the student is the availability of over 1,300 plugins available to extend the functionality of the LMS.

Schoology is another full-featured LMS. One area where Schoology really shines, however, is the number of built-in integrations, everything from YouTube to Google Drive and Dropbox, making it easier for the student to have these tools directly within the system.

Canvas is noted to be an easy-to-use interface and open source LMS, meaning it has the advantage of being free. However, many institutions do not take advantage of this free LMS primarily because of the back-end costs or the time the institution needs to spend setting up and providing ongoing management of the system. For the learner, if the institution uses Canvas, you may want to check into IT support available to you as a student. Canvas has learned from Blackboard and Moodle and tries to fill in gaps left by these two leading players. This LMS places immense emphasis on being user friendly and making communication easier and faster between educators and learners. It has a comprehensive dashboard and allows educators to offer feedback, merge various channels of education, and track students' progress seamlessly. For the student, one appealing feature is being able to combine their Canvas LMS account with their social media accounts.

Whichever LMS the institution uses, there are features that are common on most LMSs that students should be able to ask about, such as the following:

- Ability to create an educational workflow that makes sense for different environments including blended learning
- Allows for collaboration within the system – both instructor with students and students with students
- Has the ability to create, administer and score tests
- Generates reports for students, teachers, and administrators
- Integrates with common classroom tools such as Google Apps
- Enables mobile access, a key feature for college students who regularly use a smartphone
- Hosts educational content within the LMS
- Sets and tracks individual student goals
- Offers live video conferencing

"Students do not learn much just sitting in classes listening to teachers, memorizing prepackaged assignments, and spitting out answers. They must talk about what they are learning, write reflectively about it, relate it to past experiences, and apply it to their daily lives. They must make what they learn part of themselves"

Arthur W. Chickering and Stephen C. Ehrmann

8

Determine Your Learning Style

WHAT IS A LEARNING STYLE?

There are many senses our brains use to receive and process information. Some are more effective for capturing and retaining information than others and different circumstances and individuals best process information in different ways. Each person has different learning preferences and styles that benefit them. In fact, everyone's approach to learning is based on a complex mix of strengths and preferences. Each of us absorbs and applies new concepts, skills and information in different ways at different times. After all, how we learn depends a great deal on what we're learning. And our preferred learning techniques might not, in fact, be the most useful. Despite this, many scientists, psychologists and education experts have tried to identify distinct, innate "learning styles."

A learning style is an individual's approach to learning based on strengths, weaknesses, and preferences. Knowing your learning style and combination is important if you want to achieve to the best of your ability for processing information. You are a unique learner. No one else learns in the exact same way you do. There are many benefits to discovering how you process information best. Some learn best by listening, some by observing every step, while others must do it to learn it. The fact is that individuals need all three modalities to truly commit information to memory: visual, auditory, and kinesthetic. While most are typically stronger in one area than another, the trick is figuring out your preferred modality and capitalizing on these strengths. While some may find they even have a dominant learning style, others may find that they prefer different learning styles in different circumstances. Discovering how you process information may assist you in formulating strategies for better studying and learning in the classroom and improve the rate and quality of your learning.

BENEFITS OF IDENTIFYING YOUR PREDOMINANT LEARNING STYLE

There are academic, personal and professional benefits for identifying your learning style as follows:

Academic

- Gives you a head start and maximizes your learning potential
- Enables you to succeed in school, college, university
- Gives you customized techniques to score better on tests and exams
- Allows you to learn "your way" – through your own best strategies
- Shows you how to overcome the limitations of poor instructors
- Reduces the stress and frustration of learning experiences
- Expands your existing learning and studying strategies

Personal

- Increases your self-confidence
- Improves your self-image
- Teaches you how to use your brain best
- Gives your insight into your strengths, weaknesses, and habits
- Enables you to enjoy any learning process
- Inspires greater curiosity and motivation for lifelong learning
- Shows you how to take advantage of your natural skills and inclinations

Professional

- Enables you to stay up-to-date professionally
- Gives you an edge over your competitors
- Allows you to manage teams more effectively
- Guides you in delivering effective presentations to diverse audiences
- Improves your persuasive and sales skills

- Helps you improve cooperation among colleagues

- Translates learning power into earning power

It is important to know that there is no right or wrong learning style. Each style has advantages and disadvantages. Knowing your learning style is not meant to limit you but to expand you by helping you to work, learn and live more efficiently.

VARK Theory

One popular theory, the VARK model, identifies four primary types of learners: visual, auditory, reading/writing, and kinesthetic. Each learning type responds best to a different method of teaching. In the VARK model, there are strengths, weaknesses and preferences in each of the modalities. The most effective learning utilizes all three in combination.

The VAK model was initially popular and widely applied; however, many people took it to mean that learners could be classified by a single modality, such as a "visual learner," for example, with little room for maneuver. The VARK model differentiates learning strengths by the following criteria:

- Visual (spatial): You prefer using pictures, images, and spatial understanding.

- Aural (auditory-musical): You prefer using sound and music.

- Verbal (linguistic): You prefer using words, both in speech and writing.

- Physical (kinesthetic): You prefer using your body, hands and sense of touch.

It is also important to note that, while out of the scope of this book, there are also many other indexes, influential models and theories in addition to VARK that help learners determine the best way to for them to learn and comprehend new information. A few of these indexes are described briefly below.

Other Indexes for Determining Learning Style

David Kolb and Experiential Learning

David Kolb's model of experiential learning stated that we learn continually and, in the process, build particular strengths. Those strengths were said to give rise to personal preferences, which Kolb described in terms of four learning styles: Accommodating, Converging, Diverging, and Assimilating. As Kolb saw it, accommodators were "hands-on" types, keen to learn from real experience. Convergers were supposed to deal better with abstract ideas but still liked to end up with concrete results. They understood theories but wanted to test them out in practice. Divergers tended to use personal experiences and practical ideas to formulate theories that they could apply more widely. Assimilators, according to Kolb, were most comfortable working with abstract concepts. They extended their understanding by developing new theories of their own.

Kolb said that it was beneficial to know which type of learner you were in order to play to your strengths and believed that educators and trainers could tailor their teaching methods to different people's learning styles.

ANTHONY GREGORC'S MIND STYLES

Anthony Gregorc and Kathleen Butler went into more detail about how we think and how this might affect the way we learn. This theory put us all on a spectrum between concrete and abstract thinking and between sequential and random ordering of our thoughts. Concrete perceptions happen through the senses, while abstract perceptions deal with ideas. Sequential thinking arranges information in a logical, linear way, while a random approach is multidirectional and unpredictable. In Gregorc's model, our strengths and weaknesses in each of these areas determined our individual learning style.

THE LEARNING STYLES TASK FORCE

In the 1980s, American educationalists were still trying to find out as much as they could about learning styles to help teachers achieve the best possible results. The National Association of Secondary School Principals (NASSP) formed a research "task force" and proposed additional factors that might affect someone's ability to learn. These included the way study was organized, levels of motivation, and even the time of day when learning took place. They divided learning styles into three categories: Cognitive, Affective and Physiological. Cognitive is how we think, how we organize and retain information, and how we learn from our experiences. Affective is our attitudes and motivations and how they impact our approach to learning. Physiological is a variety of factors based on our health, well-being, and the environment in which we learn.

THE INDEX OF LEARNING STYLES

Various related questionnaires and tests quickly came into use, aimed at helping people to identify their personal learning style. One of the most popular was based on The

Index of Learning Styles™, developed by Dr. Richard Felder and Barbara Soloman in the late 1980s. The questionnaire considered four dimensions: Sensory/Intuitive, Visual/Verbal, Active/Reflective, and Sequential/Global. The theory was that we're all somewhere on a "continuum" for each of them. Neither extreme was said to be "good" or "bad." Instead, we would do best by drawing on both ends of the spectrum. Questionnaires like this promised to define anyone's learning style so that they could address any "imbalances" and learn in the ways that would benefit them most.

There are many learning assessments available online where can take to determine your learning style including one for the VARK theory located here https://vark-learn.com/the-vark-questionnaire/. One of my favorites is a short 20-question test found on EducationPlanner.org at http://www.educationplanner.org/students/self-assessments/learning-styles.shtml

Or Collaborative for Student Achievement

https://secure.casa.colostate.edu/applications/learningstyles/quiz.aspx

Or you can try this basic one below. Take a few minutes to complete this Learning Styles Self-Assessment. The answers may surprise you.

Online Learning Made Easy and Effective

Learning Styles Self-Assessment

1. In order to memorize information, such as the spelling of a difficult word or locker combination, you:

a. Practice repeatedly.

b. Recite the word or numbers aloud.

c. Visualize the word or numbers in your head.

2. When you want to learn new song lyrics, you:

a. Dance around and play air guitar to the beat.

b. Sing along to the radio.

c. Download the lyrics and read them.

3. While you study, you like to:

a. Walk around and review your notes.

b. Discuss the material with your parents or friends.

c. Read your notes or textbook independently.

4. When preparing to go somewhere new, you prefer to:

Determine Your Learning Style

a. Walk, drive, or bike the route ahead of time.

b. Listen to someone tell you how to get there.

c. Look at a map.

5. When you get a new gadget that needs to be assembled, you:

a. Just start putting it together.

b. Ask someone to read you the directions.

c. Read all of the steps before you begin.

6. If you have to work on a project with others, you would rather:

a. Help to build and construct a model.

b. Participate in group discussions and brainstorm ideas.

c. Draw graphs or scribe group notes.

7. You tend to like classes that include:

a. Hands-on experiments.

b. Many lectures.

c. Reading assignments.

8. When studying a play in English class, you prefer to:

a. Act it out.

b. Listen to the play read by others.

c. Read the play silently to yourself.

9. When you are able to choose a project and present it to your class, you'd rather:

a. Create a working replica.

b. Give a presentation.

c. Create a poster.

10. When you are distracted, you most often find yourself:

a. Fidgeting or playing with your pencil.

b. Listening to or participating in conversations.

c. Doodling on your notebook paper.

11. When you work at solving a challenging problem, do you:

a. Make a model of the problem or walk through all of the steps in your mind?

b. Call a few friends or talk to an expert for advice?

c. Create a list of the steps you need to take and check them off as they are done?

Once you have finished this assessment, add up the number of a's, b's, and c's. Tally your answers to have a snapshot of how you learn best! If you answered mostly "a", you are primarily a kinesthetic learner. If you answered mostly "b", you are an auditory learner, and if you answered mostly "c", you are largely a visual learner. Now that you know the way you learn best, it is time to put that information to good use.

"When it comes to eLearning, content means everything. If eLearning content is not masterfully designed, all the rest will just go down the drain"

Christopher Pappas

9

Learning Styles and Study Strategies

Learning style has to do with how people bring new information into their knowledge base. Knowing your learning style enables you to use your strengths as you study for courses. We will now discuss study strategies based on your predominant learning style.

VISUAL LEARNING STYLE

Are you one of those people who closes your eyes to envision the exact location of where you left your car keys? Do you bring up mental imagery when you are trying to remember what you did last Friday afternoon? Do you remember the cover of every book you have ever read? Do you have a photographic or near-photographic memory? Perhaps you are one of those people with the visual learning style.

Visual learners are those who process and retain information best when they can see it. Visual learners often prefer to sit in the front of the class and "watch" the lecture closely. Often, these students will find that information makes more sense when it is explained with the aid of a chart or illustration.

As a visual learner, you are usually neat and clean. You often close your eyes to visualize or remember something, and you will find something to watch if you become bored. You may have difficulty with spoken directions and may be easily distracted by sounds. You are attracted to color and to spoken language (like stories) that is rich in imagery.

What Is Visual Learning Style?

Visual learning is a learning style that was popularized by Neil D. Fleming in his VARK model of learning. The visual learning style means that people need to see information to learn it, and this "seeing" takes many forms from spatial awareness to photographic memory, color/tone, brightness/contrast, and other visual information. Naturally, a classroom is a very good place for a visual learner to learn. Teachers use overheads, the chalkboard, pictures, graphs, maps, and many other visual items to entice a visual learner into knowledge. But finding these methods of teaching is a challenge with online learning.

If you are a visual learner, you learn by reading or seeing pictures. You understand and remember things by sight. You can picture what you are learning in your head, and you learn best by using methods that are primarily visual. You like to see what you are learning.

STRENGTHS OF VISUAL LEARNERS

Visual learners typically do well in a typical classroom setting where there many are visuals—whiteboards, handouts, photos, and so on. These students have many strengths that can boost their performances in school. Here are just a few of the strengths of this learning type:

- Instinctively follows directions
- Easily visualizes objects
- Has a great sense of balance and alignment
- Is an excellent organizer
- Has a strong sense of color and is very color-oriented

- Can see the passage from a page in a book in his or her mind
- Notices minute similarities and differences between objects and people easily
- Can envision imagery easily
- Good at spelling and grammar
- Comprehends charts and graphs quickly
- Able to convey complex ideas visually
- Good at sign language and other visual communication
- Creative; may enjoy art or writing

STRATEGIES FOR THE VISUAL LEARNING STUDENT (LEARNS BEST BY SEEING)

- Try to work in a quiet place. Some visual learners like soft music in the background.
- Most visual learners learn best alone.
- When studying, take many notes and write down lots of details.

- When trying to learn material by writing out notes, cover your notes then rewrite them. Rewriting will help you remember better.

- Use color to highlight main ideas.

- Before reading a chapter or a book, preview it first by scanning the pictures, headings, terms in bold and so on.

- When creating flashcards, always add a picture cue to aide memory.

SPECIFIC STRATEGIES OF VISUAL LEARNERS FOR STUDYING

If you are a visual learner you may find these things helpful studying for a test. Visual learners need things in front of them to help solidify them in their brains, so do not try to go it alone when listening to lectures or studying for your next midterm. Integrate the following into your study routine:

- Formatting your notes using symbols, flow charts, diagrams or different colors will help you remember the connections between different ideas when you review them later. Color-code your notes, vocabulary words, and textbook. Visual learners will be able to better remember concepts through spatial and colored representations.

- Be sure to read the diagrams, maps, and other visuals that go along with text to help you remember it.

- Make to-do lists in an agenda.

- Study in solitude. You need to see things to remember them and often any noise will distract you.

- Sit near the front so you're better able to see everything.

- Use outlines and concept maps to organize your notes. Rewrite your notes replacing words with as many symbols, pictures, or drawings as possible. Create visual study aids in multiple colors.

- For a webinar or narrated presentation look for speakers' gestures or facial expressions. You will be able to better remember ideas if you can associate them with a specific movement or look of the professor.

- If your professor presents ideas in a chart format, try to copy this rather than writing out all the information in sentences.

- For PowerPoint presentations and videos, do not zone out when videos or PowerPoints are turned on.

Remember that the visual stimuli in these media will allow you to better remember the information.

- After reviewing the lesson, try redrawing your notes from memory. Do not just focus on the content but also the layout of the page. This will help reinforce the spatial and content connections on the page.

- Write out potential essay questions or test questions to help you see what your answers will look like.

How Best to Work with Teachers

When in an online learning program, try to communicate to your professor your learning style and where appropriate use this visual learning to improve your comprehension, retention, and concentration.

- **Ask for a demonstration.**

Visual learners need to see how something is done. Whenever possible, ask your instructor for a visual demonstration. Once you see the concept or principle in action, you will have an easier time understanding it and recalling it later.

- **Request handouts.**

Before the lesson begins, either access or ask the teacher if there is a handout you can review during the lecture. Handouts will help you keep track of the information being presented in the lecture.

- **Incorporate white space in your notes.**

White space is important for visual learners. When too much information is crammed together, it becomes difficult to read. Think of white space as an organizational tool like any other and use it to separate information in your notes.

- **Draw symbols and pictures.**

Use symbols like exclamation points (for important information), question marks (for information that is confusing or that you need to study further) and stars (for information you understand fully). In addition, consider illustrating complex concepts or processes.

- **Use flashcards.**

Flashcards can help you remember key terms and vocabulary words. Create a set of flashcards and illustrate them with relevant pictures and symbols to boost your retention.

- **Create graphs and charts.**

If you are learning information that can be organized as a graph or chart, take the time to make one. No need to be fancy—just scribble it in the margins of your notebook. Seeing information in this structured format will help you remember it.

- **Make outlines.**

Outlines are an excellent organizational tool for the visual learner. In an outline, you can structure a large amount of information using headings, subheadings, and bullet points. Outline chapters as you read, and then review your outlines when preparing for exams.

- **Write your own practice test.**

When you make your own practice test, you get to see the relevant test information right in front of you, which is a big help for visual learners. Use study guides, chapter notes, and relevant class assignments to put your original practice test together.

- Remember that you need to see things, not just hear things, to learn well.

Try to visualize things that you hear or things that are read to you.

Auditory Learning Style

Auditory learners learn best while they are actively listening. Auditory learners find conventional study practices, such as making notes directly from a textbook, not terribly effective. They much prefer to ingest information through audio or video clips or by discussing a topic.

If you are an auditory learner, you learn by hearing and listening. You understand and remember things you have heard. You store information by the way it sounds, and you have an easier time understanding spoken instructions than written ones. You often learn by reading aloud because you must hear it or speak it in order to know it. As an auditory learner, you probably hum or talk to yourself or others if you become bored. People may think you are not paying attention, even though you may be hearing and understanding everything that is being said.

The following are traits for auditory learning. See if they sound familiar to you. You may be an auditory learner if you are someone who:

- Likes to read to yourself aloud.

- Is not afraid to speak in class.

- Likes oral reports.

- Is good at explaining.
- Remembers names.
- Notices sound effects in movies.
- Enjoys music.
- Is good at grammar and foreign languages.
- Reads slowly.
- Follows spoken directions well.
- Cannot keep quiet for long periods.
- Enjoys acting, being on stage.
- Is good in study groups.

For the auditory learner there are things you can do to learn better. Remember that you need to **hear** things, not just see things, in order to learn well.

- Sit where you can hear.
- Have your hearing checked on a regular basis.
- Use flashcards to learn new words; read them aloud.
- Read stories, assignments, or directions aloud.
- Record yourself spelling words and then listen to the recording.

- Have test questions read to you aloud.
- Study new material by reading it aloud.
- Use word association to remember facts and lines.
- Record lectures and watch videos.
- Repeat facts with eyes closed.
- Participate in group discussions.
- Use audiotapes for language practice.
- Tape notes after writing them.

The worst test type for auditory learners is reading passages and writing answers about them in a timed test. Auditory Learners are good at writing responses to lectures they have heard. They are also good at oral exams. The online environment may not be the best fit for you. Online classes rely heavily on reading and visual communication. Be sure to research the delivery methods of an online course or program before enrolling. If in an online class, you must be prepared to engage on a regular basis with both the instructor and the other students, which will help you get the most out of your online course. Push yourself to be communicative.

STRATEGIES FOR THE AUDITORY LEARNER (LEARNS BEST BY HEARING)

- Study with a friend, parent, or group so you can discuss and hear the information.

- Recite aloud the information you want to remember several times.

- Make your own tapes of important points you want to remember and listen to them repeatedly. This is especially useful for learning material for tests.

- When doing math calculations, use grid paper to help you set your sums out correctly and in their correct columns.

TACTILE LEARNER OR KINESTHETIC LEARNER

If you are a tactile or kinesthetic learner, you learn by touching and doing. You understand and remember things through physical movement. You are a "hands-on" learner who prefers to touch, move, build, or draw what you learn, and you tend to learn better when some type of physical activity is involved. You need to be active and take frequent breaks; you often speak with your hands and with gestures, and you may have difficulty sitting still.

As a tactile learner, you like to take things apart and put them back together, and you tend to find reasons to tinker or move around when you become bored. You may be very well coordinated and have good athletic ability. You can easily remember things that were done but may have difficulty remembering what you saw or heard in the process. You often communicate by touching, and you appreciate physically expressed forms of encouragement, such as a pat on the back.

Here are some things that tactile learners can do to learn better:

- Participate in activities that involve touching, building, moving, or drawing.

- Do many hands-on activities like completing art projects, taking walks, or acting out stories.

- It is OK to chew gum, walk around, or rock in a chair while reading or studying.

- Use flashcards and arrange them in groups to show relationships between ideas.

- Trace words with your finger to learn spelling (finger spelling).

- Take frequent breaks during reading or studying

periods (frequent but not long).

- It is OK to tap a pencil, shake your foot, or hold on to something while learning.

- Use a computer to reinforce learning through the sense of touch.

Remember that you learn best by doing, not just by reading, seeing, or hearing.

Strategies for the Kinesthetic Learner
(Learns best by doing "hands on")

- Pace or walk around while referencing your notes and reciting to yourself.

- If you need to fidget, try doing so in a way that will not disturb others. Use the Tangle Jr., Wikki Sticks, or a stress ball.

- You might not study best while at a desk. Try lying on your stomach or back on a comfortable lounge chair.

- Studying with music in the background might suit you (instrumental music is best – as opposed to heavily rhythm-based music).

- While studying, take frequent breaks. A reasonable schedule would be 20–30 minutes of study, and five minutes of break time.

Classroom strategies for kinesthetic learners should include choose instructors who use real-life examples and applications or hands-on approaches. They should keep their desks clear of distracting objects and sit in a part of the classroom that offers the fewest distractions. Kinesthetic learners should always take notes, draw what they are learning whenever possible, and use a consistent color-coding system while taking notes.

For study strategies, kinesthetic learners should practice, practice, and practice. They can also work in a study group or use a tutor to develop models, experiments, and study aids. When using flashcards, kinesthetic learners can organize them spatially by grouping or categorizing them or create a moveable concept map from notes. These learners should always divide work into short study sessions with a break or reward in between them. Another strategy is for kinesthetic learners to refine and expand notes by adding color-coded examples. Finally, kinesthetic learners should take practice exams in an exam-like setting to create a physical memory that is tied to content.

Test-taking strategies for the kinesthetic learner include performing a data dump as soon as they get the test and adding to it as needed. They can chew gum to create movement! If they are having trouble remaining focused, they should get up and stretch or walk around periodically (if allowed!). Drawing or doodling while trying to recall information or recalling what they were doing or the movements they made while studying the material is also effective.

"Online learning is not the next big thing, it is the now big thing"

Donna J. Abernathy

10

Time Management Tips for the Online Student

One of the misconceptions about online college classes is that they do not require the same kind of time-management or planning skills that on-campus classes require. Taking college classes online offers flexibility and convenience, but there are still deadlines to meet and time requirements that students must satisfy. Since an online student does have more flexibility, it can be easier to plan for online classes and online exams. But every online student should take the time to master the time-management skills that will take advantage of the convenience of online learning while allowing the student to maximize their education. Regardless of your age, gender, working status, or other factors, time is one of the most important resources you have. Everything you ever hope to do or accomplish in your lifetime will take some amount of time. This is something that's especially relevant to students who are studying online. Because students are in control of their own learning and pace, they need to understand how to manage their time well to make enough room for their online courses and the rest of their responsibilities.

Why Do Online Students Need Time Management?

It's easy not to take online learning seriously. With regular classroom learning, students have a specific place they need to be at a specific time. But learning online requires students to set aside some time on their own to study and go through the lessons. This requires discipline and a real understanding of how to wisely use time throughout the day. The truth is that time is just like any other finite resource. If you don't learn how to manage time wisely, you won't be able to get things done as efficiently as possible; you may miss out on meeting your goals, fail to study often enough, and get too far behind on your lessons. Even if students don't have those specific problems, time management is also about helping them avoid stress while juggling everything.

If students are always wishing they had more hours in the day and don't know where all their time went, or feel stressed by everything they need to do, learning time management might be a solution to all of those problems. Good time-management strategies for online college students can reduce the stress that comes with trying to balance getting an education with taking care of other responsibilities.

CAN ANYONE LEARN TO MANAGE THEIR TIME BETTER?

Students may wonder if they can manage their time better. While some people may be naturally gifted in organizing themselves, time management is a skill that can be taught and learned. It's the same as any other resource management. Students will need to put in a little time investment at the beginning to plan and strategize how to use their time efficiently. If students are sufficiently diligent to learn this skill well, this little investment will help reap enormous benefits in online learning by making them more efficient and less stressed.

It's useful to learn time management sooner rather than later. Take this skill seriously. Learning time management can keep students on top of their classwork, help them stay ahead of assignment deadlines, and free up some extra time they didn't know they had for extra studying or relaxing. It's something anyone anywhere can learn at any point in their life, even they've never been good at it before.

Learning Simple Time Management

If time management is a skill, how is it learned? The basic concepts of time management are easy to grasp but difficult to put into practice consistently in your life. You'll need these intrinsic resources if you want to succeed:

Persistence

Students need to be consistent in their use of time. It will take persistence to force themselves to use their time as they had planned rather than reverting to old habits.

Dedication

Without a strong dedication to learning time management principles, students cannot hope to train themselves in time management skills. Time management isn't something anyone can learn a little bit about and move on. Rather it requires willingness to practice it constantly until it becomes second nature.

MOTIVATION

Students can set a goal in mind that will push them towards better time management practices. Use success and completion of your online learning to motivate you forward, because accomplishments in learning can be a very strong motivator.

One issue many people encounter is trying to do too much at once. Because time management is a very basic concept that's easy to grasp intellectually, it's easy to assume that you can just start practicing it immediately. Students may reorganize their entire schedule, set their alarm for earlier, and plan every detail of when they are going to go through coursework or study in the coming days; but taking such a large step at one time is unlikely to end well if it is too different from the way you normally do things. By trying to do too much at once, students are setting themselves up for failure. It's better for students to start small and work their way up, as they would with any other skill they are learning.

How to Manage Your Commuting Time to Improve Your eLearning

One simple way to start is by using time you may not think about to do simple tasks. For example, if students are doing an online course, they may be able to find some time to listen to course materials while they are commuting to and from their daily responsibilities.

Your commute may not seem long, but it's an extra 30 minutes – 1 hour daily that is otherwise empty and this can make a big difference. Students who are driving can put on a podcast from their professor or listen to an audio textbook covering the topic. If students are sharing a commute, they may be able to ask each other to quiz them on the materials they've been learning to help them stay on top of new information.

Online students who use public transport have more of an advantage because they can use that time to do a lot more. Students can bring a device that has access to data and knock out some of the online coursework on the way to and from work or other daily activities or bring a text book and keep refreshed on whatever they are learning.

The point of managing time to include activities during your commute is not to waste any of your free time. Commuting is a daily activity for most people, and instead of wasting it staring at a phone screen or listening to music on the radio, students can harness that time to improve their online learning experience and become a better student with one simple change.

TIME MANAGEMENT – FINAL THOUGHTS

The better students are with managing their time, the easier it is to achieve their goals. This is especially important for online students, who are often working full time, taking care of family, or juggling other commitments. Good time management allows you to accomplish more in a shorter period of time, which leads to more free time, which lets you take advantage of learning opportunities, lowers your stress, and helps you focus, which leads to more career success. Each benefit of time management improves another aspect of your life.

When it comes to getting your assignments in on time, a good time-management tactic is to become intimately familiar with the structure of your classes and the work that will be required of you. When you get your course outlines, read them completely and develop an understanding of what will be expected of you. Include your assignments on your calendar, and avoid leaving things until their deadline. As your class covers material relevant to your assignments, that is the time to start your assignments. Always plan on completing your assignments at least three days prior to their due dates and you will start to develop the good habits you need to be successful with an online program.

A student's hectic schedule, combined with daily distractions, can easily get in the way of finishing tasks. Another time management hack to use when it comes to finding time for your classes is being proactive. When students get their semester schedule, they should take a proactive approach to planning their week around attending their classes. Set aside time each week to complete lectures and take part in any required activities. The most successful online students know how to set aside time to focus. This includes having a consistent time and workspace, tuning out distractions and avoiding surfing the internet. Despite the flexibility in being an online student, it is important to have frequent engagement with their studies throughout the week. Provide plenty of time to space out required readings, assignments and online discussions. Consider purchasing a calendar to plan your daily and weekly assignments, highlighting:

- Assignments due, including drafts and final submissions

- Activities related to the program, such as study group meetups or on-campus networking events

- Virtual or in-person office hours with professors and advisors

Discussion Board Posting Time Management – Sample of Typical Week

When managing your discussion board postings and assignments, here is a sample schedule of what a typical week might look like:

Monday	Begin required readings and multimedia
Tuesday	Continue reviewing materials
Wednesday	Post to discussion forum and begin assignments
Thursday	Continue posting and working on assignments
Friday	Read and respond to posts and work on assignments
Saturday	Read and respond to posts and finish assignments
Sunday	Check your work and submit assignments

"My true inspiration is my desire to share online learning strategies to students to help them reach their educational goal and cultivate their greatness"

Terris R. Moss, PhD, Educator, Author, Speaker

11

Strategies for the Online Learner

FRONT-LOAD YOUR WORK

A big difference between learning face-to-face and online is the "front-loading" required. Your professor will need to plan and post everything before the course even opens. Students who want to do well in online courses should front-load their work as much as possible. Developing a strategy for completing deliverables on time includes reading the syllabus, reviewing assignment guidelines, and taking note of the deadlines as soon as you can access the course page. Look at which days of the week assignments are due. When does your work-life schedule allow you to do them? Can you work ahead on anything now to save you time later in the course when things might be more hectic?

ASK LOTS OF QUESTIONS

Unfortunately, there may be unanswered questions in online courses. When you are face-to-face and a question comes up you can ask it right away. Sometimes a classmate asks the question first. Either way, you get an answer before you leave. Without a classroom, however, it is up to you to ask questions—immediately. Professors post a syllabus that should answer most questions. However, even good professors make mistakes. My suggestion is to read your syllabus very carefully. Teachers should clearly denote what they expect from their students and what students should expect from their teacher; if you are unsure of anything look back through emails or announcements. If you do not find an answer, ask the professor. The professors want you to do well, and if you are proactive, they will be responsive.

RELEASE YOUR EXTROVERT

In cyberspace, there is not a back of the room. Everyone is front row center. You need to engage in every activity and prove that you read, learned, or applied the material when you submit a post, paper, or presentation. Without a classroom, however, it is up to you to ask questions immediately. You cannot afford to wait until you are noticed in an online course.

PERCEPTION CAN BE YOUR (VIRTUAL) REALITY

Even full courses without any face-to-face interaction can feel like a small room where you talk to your peers regularly and have access to a great professor; students may feel disconnected and need to adapt to cultural differences and communication styles. Establish a connection to build with students and teachers would avoid the perception of a "faceless students". Go out of your way to make and meet new friends. Connect with others and network. But if you get caught off-guard by a school requirement, wait to ask a question until it is too late or miss a deadline, your online class can become very big and very lonely, very fast.

GET A SUPPORT SYSTEM OF FAMILY AND FRIENDS

While juggling family, work and school commitments can be a challenge, it does not have to be impossible. Have a frank discussion with family members. Sit down with your partner and discuss how they can take on more responsibilities.

The same is true for children. Explain to your children why you are pursuing an education—be it to land a job or earn more money for the family—so that they understand the importance of being supportive and giving their parent time to study. Take advantage of the time you have. For example, make every spare second count when it comes to your studies; in the car while a child finishes piano practice or waiting in the doctor's office during a doctor visit can be a great opportunity to whip out some reading materials or start studying. Try not to burden yourself with an impossible workload. Earning an online degree can be a noble goal, but it does not necessarily need to be done as fast as possible.

STAY CONNECTED

Just because students are not physically in the same location doesn't mean they cannot get to know their fellow classmates. Students should build relationships with other students by introducing themselves and engaging in online discussion boards. Making an effort to ask and answer questions to enhance understanding of the course material can build a bond with other students. Peers can be a valuable resource when preparing for exams or asking for feedback on assignments. Making connections with the other students in the online classroom could result in a built-in study group.

Reach out to your instructor to introduce yourself or ask questions, or both. They are eager to engage one-on-one with their students, whether online or in person. And if you do fall behind, speak up. Don't wait until an assignment is almost due to ask questions or report issues. Email the professor and be proactive in asking for help.

Have an Open Mind

Some online learners feel more comfortable sharing their thoughts and opinions virtually than in the classroom. Online learning provides students with the time they need to actively reflect and organize their thoughts before answering a question or making a comment. Having an open mind helps students interact with the material and fosters a more engaged and open community.

Hold Yourself Accountable

Set goals at the beginning of the semester and check in weekly. In a traditional classroom setting, students will often receive verbal or visual reminders of an assignment's upcoming due date. But without a professor actively providing reminders, it is up to the student to make sure they have allotted enough time to complete the work so they're not starting an assignment the day before it's due. If you're having trouble holding yourself responsible, you should try pairing up with a fellow classmate or enlist the help of a spouse or friend to check in as an accountability partner. By being organized, proactive, and self-aware, students can get the most from their online class even when life outside of school becomes chaotic.

"By failing to prepare, you are preparing to fail"

Benjamin Franklin

12

Strategies, Hacks and Resources for Online Learning Success

Online education can pose unique challenges and take some getting used to, especially for the new student. There will likely be a learning curve, especially for students who are not technologically perceptive. The following are some helpful tips for online college success.

TIP 1 – TREAT STUDYING LIKE A JOB

Although online courses offer flexibility in terms of when students can complete their tasks, if students treat studying as their work, they are prone to consciously choose to show up, absorb the course content available, and schedule in assessments, lectures and tasks. By setting these boundaries, students treat online classes like a job and perform tasks such as setting daily goals, making checklists and accomplishing small goals each day. Make a study plan at the beginning of each term planning a certain number of hours each day for readings and assignments leaving some flexibility for the unexpected.

Tip 2 – Make Use of Online Resources

Students should ask their instructors what the online resources are available. For example, colleges often have an online library, which offers sources for assignments. Another resource that is sometimes available is a writing center. If students need their paper corrected or just have a question on formatting, the writing center can help. Some colleges may even have virtual tutors. Students should get familiar with the school website and how to access resources such as the library, upcoming classes, website info, technical support and more. Also, students should ensure they know how to contact their school, teachers, and other people when they have a question or concern. Take time to click on each tab on the school's website to see what information is available before getting started.

Tip 3 – Check in Daily

For online classes, students only need internet access to connect to their courses. If you have an iPhone or Android device, leverage it to stay organized. Make contact every day, not necessarily doing full-blown homework, just check in to stay current. Checking into school as a daily activity makes it less overwhelming and it prevents students from being caught off guard by syllabus changes.

Tip 4 – Don't Multitask

Avoid multitasking—which can actually decrease your productivity. Focus on one assignment at a time and zero in on the specific task, whether you are studying for an exam, reading a textbook, emailing a professor, or participating in an online forum. Arrange your tasks in order of importance and pay attention to the three or four crucial tasks that require the most effort. If you need help staying focused, consider creating lists using a project management tool, such as Trello or Smartsheet, to help organize tasks. If you prefer a traditional to-do list, then check out digital notebooks like Todoist, Wunderlist, or Evernote.

Concentrate on what needs to be done in the present and avoid anything too far off. If it is a small assignment that you do not need to address for several weeks, put it on your calendar to focus on when the deadline is closer.

TIP 5 – SPEAK UP AND ASK QUESTIONS

If you struggle or fall behind, do not stay silent. It is important if you are struggling with a topic to be proactive and seek help. Many online courses have great instructors just waiting to assist you. Ask questions as soon as you have them. There is nothing worse than convincing yourself that you will eventually learn the subject and finding out a week later that you still do not understand the topic. Generally, with online classes, one week is built off the knowledge of the past week. If you do not understand week one, you will have greater difficulty in week two, and so on.

Some students are hesitant to ask for help. They start to drown; then they take drastic measures or they do not take measures at all. Either way, they end up making a mistake. Instructors may offer wiggle room with deadlines or extra credit if a situation warrants it and most online programs have teams of counselors and advisers to help you along the way; however, students need to be proactive and speak up if they are running into difficulty. Even if the course seems like a total loss, usually someone can help. Instructors do not want students to fail and may find a middle ground to rescue what can be salvaged and move forward from there.

TIP 6 – CONNECT WITH OTHERS

Online portals, discussion boards and Facebook can help find students in the same course, maybe even in your local area. Connect with peers and team up for group assessments, stay in touch and help each other with proofreading, tips and exchange of resources. Talking to other students opens my mind and keeps me motivated. An important part of the online classroom is classroom participation and discussion; posts that engage others in a back and forth aid in the conceptualization of research papers and slide presentations that are assigned as homework. Group projects lead students to collaborate using interactive cloud-based platforms, interact in real-time using web conferencing apps and produce online presentations together. Most online classes also have discussion boards integrated into their interface. Embracing these message boards not only helps students achieve academic success, but it also opens the door for the type of casual social interaction that comes naturally in a face-to-face setting.

Interact with your classmates and lecturer as though you were doing in-class learning to gain the ultimate benefits. Communication with other students is vital. In order to fully comprehend certain material, it is sometimes necessary to see another person's point of view on the subject matter. Talking to other students by messaging or posting comments can sometimes open a student's mind to other opinions or help them understand an assignment. Students learn from each other and cooperative learning is the same online as it is in any traditional college.

Ask questions and participate as much as you can. There are so many great opportunities as an online learner because the students in your class are usually from all over the United States. As a student, you can draw information and gain more knowledge and different perspectives than you may in a face-to-face classroom setting.

TIP 7 – JOIN A STUDY TEAM

While students may not physically sit next to their classmates, that does not mean they should expect to complete their degree program alone. They should expect plenty of interactions with other students, the instructor and the course content. Students should create a team of virtual friends, two to three, maybe more, and have regular discussions to pick each other's brains, see how far each is coming along with the assignments and help with any challenges anyone is facing. This can be accomplished using WhatsApp or Facebook. One of the best ways to be successful is to group together with study friends. Study friends can bounce ideas, work out task requirements, study for exams, offload when stressed, encourage, and remind one another that it will all be worth it.

TIP 8 – SET UP YOUR VIRTUAL OFFICE

Whether you study at home or in your local café, it is important to work in the optimal setting needed to complete your work. Make sure there is high-speed internet and that you are in a comfortable space with the right lighting, sound and background. For example, some people prefer to work using headphones, while others prefer silence or an ambient backdrop with people quietly chatting. Sit in a comfortable chair and make sure the lighting is not too dim. Close out your browser windows and put your phone away. Along with these elements, make sure you have all the required materials, such as textbooks and industry-specific software. Set up as much as you can ahead of time to stay on task with your coursework.

Tip 9 – Embrace Project Management Tools

Instead of trying to manage everything in your head or on a calendar, put on your project manager hat. Meeting your milestones—due dates—will be critical to your success. Take advantage of some of the following tools to help you manage your time wisely (some are specific to coursework; others you can use to organize personal life and college studies together):

- **My Homework**—this app is an option for students who want a tool solely devoted to school. No more student planners—now you can use your favorite devices to stay organized. Free and paid versions are available for iPhone, Android, Mac, PC, Kindle Fire, and Google Chrome browser.

- **Todoist**—Todoist gives users a platform where they can manage multiple tasks—school, work, personal—and assign a task to its corresponding project. Students with busy family lives or hectic work schedules can put everything in Todoist to get a clear overview of all their tasks and deadlines. Todoist can be used in a desktop browser or on a smartphone or tablet.

- **Trello**—if you enjoy a "drag and drop" environment, Trello may be the tool for you. Trello is flexible—simply organize your coursework and other projects in the way that works best for you. Use Trello board to manage schoolwork and have a list of cards for each class. When an assignment is complete, drag that card into the completed list. Trello can be used in a desktop browser or a smartphone app. A free version is available, but users can upgrade to a paid plan for more features.

Conclusion

Online Education has brought a positive impact in the lives of students and working professionals. It has provided an opportunity to take up additional courses along with their studies or job as per their convenience. Online education has also helped the faculties in the institutions to ask students to study some parts of the syllabus online, which do not require much classroom instruction. So the online study helps the faculty to save time in which they can interact with the students more. The quality of education has improved with online courses and it has become easy for students to refer to the course content at their leisure. In the era of digitalization the scope of online education is increasing even more and will be beneficial for students, professionals and also institutions.

Online Learning Made Easy and Effective

The timing has never been better for using technology to enable and improve learning at all levels, in all places, and for people of all backgrounds. From the modernization of E-rate which expansion of robust Wi-Fi Networks in nationwide schools and to the spread and adoption of openly licensed educational resources, the key pieces necessary to realize best the transformations made possible by technology in education are in place.

Although the presence of technology does not ensure equity and accessibility in learning, it has the power to lower barriers to both in ways previously impossible. No matter their perceived abilities or geographic locations, all learners can access resources, experiences, planning tools, and information that can set them on a path to acquiring expertise unimaginable a generation ago. Technology allows for greater communication, resource sharing, and improved practice so that the vision is owned by all and dedicated to helping every individual in the system improve learning for students.

Hundreds of online college programs are now available from the world's best universities and professors. However, online learning is often presented in a "one size fits all" curriculum. A scientific understanding of learning includes understanding about learning processes, learning environments, and learning styles, which contributes to learning ease and effectiveness for online students. As an online school strategist, Dr. Moss provides students with resources, strategies and professional guidance to ensure successful completion of their online college program. By designing strategies based on her students' learning styles, Dr. Moss will equip her student clients with the information they need to make their online education journey easier and more efficient.

Resources for Online Education Students

Online Education Strategic Program available for purchase at https://mossconsulting.samcart.com/products/online-education-strategies-program

Basics on Online Learning e-Book
Learn the truth about 3 myths for online education, pros and cons of each type of online learning format and learning management systems, and typical actions students must complete each week to be successful. ($45 Value)

Online Learning Easy and Effective e-Book
Learn what is a learning style, its importance and identify your predominant learning style and study strategies based on your individual learning style. ($45 Value)

13 Practical Tips for the Online Student e-Book
Learn how to manage your time, tasks and plan ahead, what resources are available to online students and how to find them and much, much more. ($45 value)

Pursuing a Degree Online Auto book available for purchase at: http://www.buybooksontheweb.com/product.aspx?ISBN=1-4958-0086-5

www.ingramcontent.com/pod-product-compliance
Lightning Source LLC
Chambersburg PA
CBHW071451080526
44587CB00014B/2068